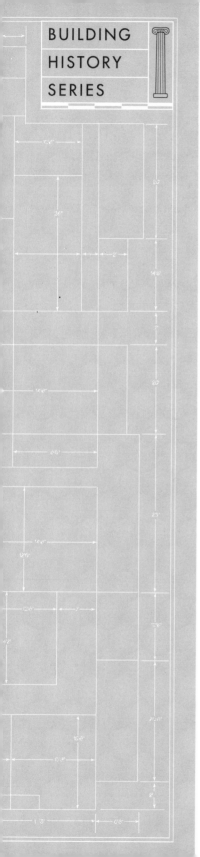

BUILDING
HISTORY
SERIES

MOUNT
RUSHMORE

BUILDING
HISTORY
SERIES

MOUNT RUSHMORE

by Judith Janda Presnall

Lucent Books, Inc., San Diego, California

I extend my thanks and appreciation to several people whose assistance added to the accuracy and interest of this book:

James G. Popovich, chief of interpretation at Mount Rushmore National Memorial in Keystone, South Dakota, who reviewed the manuscript and answered questions.

Ranger Steve Kveene of the National Park Service at Mount Rushmore, who led my husband and me to the top of the mountain.

Glenn Bradford of Rapid City, South Dakota, a Mount Rushmore carpenter during the summer of 1939, who shared his memories and experiences of working on the monument.

My husband, Lance Presnall, who accepted photography duties during the trip to the Black Hills.

Library of Congress Cataloging-in-Publication Data

Presnall, Judith, Janda.
     Mount Rushmore / by Judith Janda Presnall.
         p.   cm. — (Building history series)
     Includes bibliographical references and index.
     Summary: Examines the history of unique national monument in the Black Hills of South Dakota, Mount Rushmore, discussing financial issues, government involvement, and the actual process of carving this memorial.
     ISBN 1-56006-529-X (alk. paper)
     1. Mount Rushmore National Memorial (S.D.)—History
Juvenile literature.   [1. Mount Rushmore National Memorial
(S.D.)   2. National monuments.]   I. Title.   II. Series.
F657.R8P66   2000
978.3'93—DC21   99-31390
                                                                CIP

Printed in the U.S.A.

In memory of
Edward G. Janda
Tess M. Janda
Alice R. Presnall
Lewis F. Presnall

Contents

FOREWORD

Throughout history, as civilizations have evolved and prospered, each has produced unique buildings and architectural styles. Combining the need for both utility and artistic expression, a society's buildings, particularly its large-scale public structures, often reflect the individual character traits that distinguish it from other societies. In a very real sense, then, buildings express a society's values and unique characteristics in tangible form. As scholar Anita Abramovitz comments in her book *People and Spaces*, "Our ways of living and thinking—our habits, needs, fear of enemies, aspirations, materialistic concerns, and religious beliefs—have influenced the kinds of spaces that we build and that later surround and include us."

That specific types and styles of structures constitute an outward expression of the spirit of an individual people or era can be seen in the diverse ways that various societies have built palaces, fortresses, tombs, churches, government buildings, sports arenas, public works, and other such monuments. The ancient Greeks, for instance, were a supremely rational people who originated Western philosophy and science, including the atomic theory and the realization that the earth is a sphere. Their public buildings, epitomized by Athens's magnificent Parthenon temple, were equally rational, emphasizing order, harmony, reason, and above all, restraint.

By contrast, the Romans, who conquered and absorbed the Greek lands, were a highly practical people preoccupied with acquiring and wielding power over others. The Romans greatly admired and readily copied elements of Greek architecture, but modified and adapted them to their own needs. "Roman genius was called into action by the enormous practical needs of a world empire," wrote historian Edith Hamilton. "Rome met them magnificently. Buildings tremendous, indomitable, amphitheaters where eighty thousand could watch a spectacle, baths where three thousand could bathe at the same time."

In medieval Europe, God heavily influenced and motivated the people, and religion permeated all aspects of society, molding people's worldviews and guiding their everyday actions. That spiritual mindset is reflected in the most important medieval structure—the Gothic cathedral—which, in a sense, was a model of heavenly cities. As scholar Anne Fremantle so elegantly phrases it, the cathedrals were "harmonious elevations of stone and glass reaching up to heaven to seek and receive the light [of God]."

Our more secular modern age, in contrast, is driven by the realities of a global economy, advanced technology, and mass communications. Responding to the needs of international trade and the growth of cities housing millions of people, today's builders construct engineering marvels, among them towering skyscrapers of steel and glass, mammoth marine canals, and huge and elaborate rapid transit systems, all of which would have left their ancestors, even the Romans, awestruck.

In examining some of humanity's greatest edifices, Lucent Books' Building History series recognizes this close relationship between a society's historical character and its buildings. Each volume in the series begins with a historical sketch of the people who erected the edifice, exploring their major achievements as well as the beliefs, customs, and societal needs that dictated the variety, functions, and styles of their buildings. A detailed explanation of how the selected structure was conceived, designed, and built, to the extent that this information is known, makes up the majority of the volume.

Each volume in the Lucent Building History series also includes several special features that are useful tools for additional research. A chronology of important dates gives students an overview, at a glance, of the evolution and use of the structure described. Sidebars create a broader context by adding further details on some of the architects, engineers, and construction tools, materials, and methods that made each structure a reality, as well as the social, political, and/or religious leaders and movements that inspired its creation. Useful maps help the reader locate the nations, cities, streets, and individual structures mentioned in the text; and numerous diagrams and pictures illustrate tools and devices that bring to life various stages of construction. Finally, each volume contains two bibliographies, one for student research, the other listing works the author consulted in compiling the book.

Taken as a whole, these volumes, covering diverse ancient and modern structures, constitute not only a valuable research tool, but also a tribute to the human spirit, a fascinating exploration of the dreams, skills, ingenuity, and dogged determination of the great peoples who shaped history.

Important Dates in the Building of Mount Rushmore

1924
Historian Doane Robinson contacts sculptor Gutzon Borglum regarding a massive carving of heroes in the Black Hills of South Dakota.

1926
Borglum designs a rough model of Washington, Jefferson, Lincoln, and Roosevelt.

1930
Washington figure is dedicated.

1934
Matching-funds clause amended to provide funding for the memorial by direct government appropriation.

1929
Congress passes a bill authorizing $250,000 in matching federal funds for the Rushmore project.

| 1924 | 1926 | 1928 | 1930 | 1932 | 1934 |

1925
Borglum and son, Lincoln, choose Mount Rushmore as the site for the sculpture; Mount Rushmore is dedicated as a national memorial.

1932
Work stops due to lack of funds; the federal government grants a total of $100,000 to South Dakota.

1928
Work stops due to lack of funds.

1927
Borglum signs contract for Mount Rushmore carving; first drilling ceremony takes place; work begins.

The figures slowly emerge from the rock.

1935
Congress authorizes $200,000.

Roosevelt unveiled, 1939

1937
Lincoln figure is dedicated.

1991
President George Bush attends fiftieth anniversary along with nineteen surviving Mount Rushmore workers.

1939
Congress imposes a June 1940 deadline for completion of the memorial; Theodore Roosevelt figure is dedicated.

| 1936 | 1938 | 1940 | 1942 | 1990 | 2000 |

1938
Congress authorizes $300,000.

1998
New visitor accommodations and administrative facilities are dedicated; Gutzon Borglum's descendants bury a crypt containing historical records in the Hall of Records entranceway.

1940
Congress appropriates $86,000, the final grant for the monument.

1941
Gutzon Borglum dies in Chicago on March 6; work on the memorial is completed under Lincoln Borglum.

1936
Jefferson figure is dedicated in the presence of President Franklin D. Roosevelt.

Introduction

South Dakota's Black Hills are home to the world's largest sculpture—Mount Rushmore National Memorial. The monument consists of giant images of four presidents: George Washington, Thomas Jefferson, Abraham Lincoln, and Theodore Roosevelt. The dimensions of the carvings are overwhelming. The sixty-foot faces have noses that are twenty feet long, mouths that are eighteen feet across, and eyes that are eleven feet wide.

"The four presidents on Mount Rushmore represent the nation's finest ideals as they were shaped in our first 150 years and that we've lived by ever since,"[1] said James G. Popovich, Mount Rushmore's chief of interpretation. These principles include independence, government by the people, preservation of the union, and expansion.

JUSTIFICATION FOR A MEMORIAL

The initial reason for creating such a monument was to attract tourists to South Dakota. Thanks in large measure to Mount Rushmore, that goal was achieved. Today, tourism is second in revenue sources for South Dakota.

Patriotism was also a factor. The sculptor chosen for the project, Gutzon Borglum, saw this undertaking as a great and lasting tribute to the country he so loved. Borglum expected that the monument would not only attract tourists but would also become a symbol of American democracy. But he was unprepared for the many obstacles and stressful issues that he would encounter during its construction.

HINDRANCES

Carving the face of a mountain presented many problems. The most difficult of these was financial, and much of the Mount Rushmore story revolves around the struggle to secure funding. From Borglum's first visit to the Black Hills in 1924 to the day construction ended in 1941, money was always difficult to obtain.

Gutzon Borglum's personality created a second obstacle. Both politicians and supporters doubted that the monument could be completed within a reasonable time period and at a reasonable cost. To satisfy their skepticism, Borglum actively participated in fund-raising and in solving administrative problems. Although his flair for publicity and enthusiasm was alluring, his lack of financial keenness and his desire to be in charge of every detail caused havoc.

One of the minor obstacles was the disagreement over which Americans to include in the sculpture, but Borglum stood firm in the four presidents he chose. It was important to him that the memorial represent the spirit and principles of American geographical expansion and political development. The sculptured figures would include those who, in Borglum's estimation, contributed most to the nation's material progress and living ideals.

South Dakota's Mount Rushmore National Memorial depicts the faces of Presidents George Washington, Thomas Jefferson, Theodore Roosevelt, and Abraham Lincoln. Symbolizing America's democracy and ideals, the world's largest sculpture was shaped by Gutzon Borglum.

High above the canyon, a driller strapped in a bosun's seat braces his legs while chiseling with a jackhammer.

Some people opposed defacing nature, but they proved to be only slight irritations to Borglum. Indeed, since he believed he was creating something of great patriotic and artistic importance, he ignored anyone who did not agree with him.

THE POWER OF PEOPLE AND TOOLS

The story of Mount Rushmore is also the story of the men and women who worked on the project. From 1927 through 1941 nearly four hundred people worked on Mount Rushmore in different capacities. Some were strapped in leather harnesses while they blasted, drilled, and chipped on the six-thousand-foot high mountain. Some worked as blacksmiths, callboys, winch operators, and carpenters. Women prepared food and performed secretarial duties. The primary tools the workers used to remove over 450,000 tons of rock were dynamite and jackhammers. The immense venture, however, kept many people employed who were grateful to have a job, especially during the Great Depression.

The vast size of Mount Rushmore and the challenges it posed pleased sculptor Borglum: "There is something in sheer volume that awes and terrifies, lifts us out of ourselves, something that relates us to God and to what is greatest in our evolving universe."[2] Despite having sculpted hundreds of other statues throughout America and Europe, Borglum considered Mount Rushmore his greatest achievement. "My father was prouder of Rushmore than of anything else he did," recalls his daughter, Mary Ellis Borglum Vhay. "He always had the courage of his convictions in the simplest way—he believed anyone could do whatever they wanted if they had guts and determination."[3]

A COLOSSAL VENTURE

Three ideas provided the springboard for what would eventually become the Mount Rushmore National Memorial: carving some granite pinnacles, honoring heroic westerners in a monument, and boosting the economy of South Dakota through tourism. In 1923 Doane Robinson, historian and secretary for the South Dakota State Historical Society, conceived the idea of creating a giant outdoor sculpture honoring American heroes, but he could neither envision the nature of the completed sculpture nor the choice of subjects for it. The finished monument would, however, achieve his primary objective—to attract tourists to South Dakota.

COLOSSAL THOUGHTS

In the 1920s Americans were feeling prosperous and optimistic about the future. World War I had ended in 1918, and America and its allies were victorious. Americans, in an upbeat mood, took pride in significant accomplishments, including the tallest skyscraper, the Woolworth Building; oversized sculptures like the Lincoln Memorial; and lavish, epic movies such as *The Ten Commandments*. It was a time for big ideas to be put into action.

Since grandness was popular, Robinson thought about how he could incorporate this concept to benefit the state of South Dakota. Not only was Robinson well versed in law, poetry, and literature, but he had also been secretary of the historical society since its inception in 1901. More importantly, he enjoyed the love and respect of fellow South Dakotans; therefore, he could influence the choice of projects for drawing tourists to the state.

Robinson had read about a colossal monument at Stone Mountain near Atlanta, Georgia, that was in progress. The sculpture, honoring

Doane Robinson's main goal was to attract tourists to the state of South Dakota.

heroes of the Civil War, was being done in bas relief, meaning the figures protruded outward from the flat mountain wall. The four-hundred-foot-high and quarter-mile-long granite wall was to encase hundreds of figures. Confederate infantry, cavalry, and artillery would sweep down to converge upon huge central figures of Robert E. Lee, Stonewall Jackson, Jefferson Davis, and four other southern heroes that were yet to be chosen. Robinson wanted a comparable commemorative sculpture for South Dakota.

FINDING A SCULPTOR

Robinson studied the Black Hills of South Dakota, an area of sixty miles by one hundred miles that was filled with free-standing protrusions of granite. He envisioned carving these one-hundred-foot needles, or pinnacles, into human figures. Robinson contacted Lorado Taft, America's leading sculptor. In his December 1923 letter to Taft, Robinson described the Black Hills and enclosed a brochure that pictured the needles. He sug-

Borglum studies a projected image of his Confederate Memorial at Stone Mountain, Georgia.

gested to Taft that these needles could be carved into human figures, and he mentioned Sioux chief Red Cloud as one possible subject.

Taft replied that he was suffering from poor health, and it was unlikely that he could consider the proposal. However, since Taft did not flatly reject the idea, Robinson followed up with another letter in which he elaborated on his dream:

> Near the summit is a little park through which the highway passes. . . . It is studded with column after column of these pinnacles and in my imagination I can see all the heroes of the old west peering out from them; Lewis and Clark, [John] Fremont, Jed Smith, [Jim] Bridger, Sakaka-wea [Sacagawea], Red Cloud, and in an equestrian statue [Buffalo Bill] Cody and the overland mail.[4]

PROMOTING THE IDEA

Aware of the importance of building political support for his idea, Robinson sent a copy of his first letter to Republican senator Peter Norbeck from South Dakota. For the past twenty years Senator Norbeck had been Congress's leading advocate of park and game development in the Black Hills. He was both protective of the Black Hills's beauty and interested in attracting tourist dollars to his home state. Norbeck reacted cautiously to Robinson's idea, saying "It is a new suggestion entirely: I had never thought of it."[5]

A month later, in January 1924, Robinson first publicly proposed his idea of carving a colossal monument in the Black Hills during a speech in Huron, South Dakota, to a group promoting state tourism. The purpose of the carvings, Robinson told the Black and Yellow Trail Association, was to draw visitors to South Dakota; despite their natural scenic beauty, the Black Hills were not attracting enough tourists. "Tourists soon get fed up on scenery unless it has something of special interest connected with it to make it impressive,"[6] Robinson asserted.

Word spread quickly throughout the state. About a week after that meeting, the Associated Press carried a story from Pierre, South Dakota, discussing Robinson's plan:

> A definite project of converting a group of Black Hills "Needles" into massive and spectacular figures of sculpture emblematic of the outstanding historical life of the

Historian Doane Robinson suggested that these granite needles, carved into heroic figures such as Sioux chief Red Cloud, Lewis and Clark, and Buffalo Bill Cody, would attract tourists to South Dakota. The stone, however, was found unsuitable for carving.

state, has been conceived by Doane Robinson. Hundreds of visitors would be drawn into the state to view such a landmark.[7]

PROS AND CONS

Once the public got wind of a proposed carving in the Black Hills, various opinions were expressed. Negative comments came in the form of steaming personal letters and barbed editorials. In 1924 environmentalist groups did not have a name, but they did exist. Their members' comments included, "Why desecrate a noble work of nature with a puny work of man?" and "Statuary among the Needles would be as ridiculous as keeping a cow in the Capitol rotunda."[8]

Even newspapers on the other side of the state expressed their disapproval. The Yankton *Press and Dakotan* declared that

the idea is not likely to meet with unanimous favor. . . .
We who live out on the plains are quite satisfied with the

beauties of our great Black Hills as bequeathed to us by nature. . . . It would seem rather presumptuous to attempt to improve on the scenic beauties . . . however accomplished the artist or perfect the design.[9]

One Black Hills resident, Cora B. Johnson, censured the idea bitterly in a letter to South Dakota's *Hot Springs Star:* "We view with alarm Doane Robinson's proposal to carve the Needles into statues. Man makes statues but God made the Needles. Let them alone."[10]

Robinson, however, insisted that he did *not* intend to desecrate the hills. He intended only to use a little corner of the Needles for a carved display that would commemorate the heroes of the Old West and at the same time bring tourist dollars to Dakota and the Black Hills. Despite the negative comments, Robinson was encouraged by favorable responses from the many editors, individuals, and commercial clubs interested in increasing profits from tourists. The Sioux Falls *Daily Argus Leader,* South Dakota's largest newspaper, enthusiastically supported the idea.

NEXT CHOICE: SCULPTOR GUTZON BORGLUM

As time wore on, sculptor Taft showed no signs of changing his mind. So on August 20, 1924, Robinson wrote to Gutzon Borglum, the sculptor working on Georgia's Stone Mountain:

Dear Mr. Borglum:

In the vicinity of Harney Peak in the Black Hills of South Dakota are opportunities for heroic sculpture of unusual character. Would it be possible for you to design and supervise a massive sculpture there? The proposal has not passed beyond mere suggestion, but if it would be possible for you to undertake the matter I feel quite sure we could arrange to finance such an enterprise. I should be glad to hear from you at your convenience.

Faithfully,
Doane Robinson, Supt.[11]

This letter arrived at an opportune time. Borglum's work on the Stone Mountain memorial had proved that it was indeed possible to carve mountains. Moreover, although Borglum was enjoying immense publicity generated by the project, a serious controversy was brewing. Consequently, Borglum was happy to undertake a backup project.

After exchanging several telegrams, Borglum and Robinson agreed to meet in September. Robinson was excited at the prospect of Borglum's visit and the advancement of his idea for a sculpture in South Dakota. But who was Gutzon Borglum? Robinson only knew that the man was a "daring, imaginative, and intensely patriotic artist who might implement his vision."[12]

THE STORY OF GUTZON BORGLUM

John Gutzon de la Mothe Borglum was born in the Idaho Territory on March 25, 1867, of Danish parents. Borglum's family had

Gutzon Borglum with his carving of Abraham Lincoln. The president's distinctive features made him a favorite subject of many sculptors.

lived in several states including Idaho, Utah, Missouri, Nebraska, and California. Borglum showed artistic talent during his childhood, especially in drawing western subjects such as cowboys, horses, and Indians. As a teenager, Borglum found restrictions at home and at school distasteful, so he ran away, ending up in San Francisco.

There, Borglum studied art. At age twenty-two he married forty-year-old Elizabeth "Lisa" Putnam, a still-life painter and teacher. During their nineteen-year marriage, Putnam devoted her life to furthering Borglum's art interests and career. After a move to Europe to study in Paris, London, and Spain, Borglum diversified his craft to include sculpting. During this time, however, his marriage foundered and ended in divorce.

After the failure of his first marriage, Borglum married Mary Montgomery in 1908. Their marriage produced two children, James Lincoln in 1912 and Mary Ellis in 1916. By this time Borglum had abandoned other art forms and considered himself exclusively a sculptor. His favorite subjects to sculpt were horses and humans, especially focusing on their faces.

At the time Doane Robinson contacted him, Borglum had sculpted hundreds of pieces, which were on display throughout

CARVING THE HUMAN FACE

In *Six Wars at a Time: The Life and Times of Gutzon Borglum, Sculptor of Mount Rushmore,* Howard Shaff and Audrey Karl Shaff quote an article that Gutzon Borglum wrote for the New York *American-Examiner.* In "How Your Face Betrays You," Borglum comments on his small sculptured figure of Nero, which he created in 1904.

> In moulding the mouth of Nero I used my observation of men of his type. His mouth is full and loose; its thickness expresses sensuality and grossness. He had little upper lip—in fact, according to historians, his lower lip closed over his upper. His mouth was unquestionably of his own creation; its fullness and looseness were consciously molded by a mind which reveled in gross things. . . . More eloquent than any characteristic, however, is the human face. It expresses goodness; it reveals evil; it also shows cunning, selfishness, just as clearly as generosity and honesty.

the United States. Among others, Borglum's works include over one hundred figures for the Cathedral of St. John the Divine in New York City; a major bronze of stampeding horses, the *Mares of Diomedes,* owned by the Metropolitan Museum of Art in New York City; and one of his largest and finest paintings, *Staging over the Sierra Madres* for the Joslyn Museum in Omaha, Nebraska. He also sculpted several pieces portraying Abraham Lincoln, including a marble portrait in the Capitol Building in Washington, D.C., and a bronze *Seated Lincoln* in front of the courthouse in Newark, New Jersey.

In addition to a fondness for grand projects, the sculptor had a profound sense of patriotism. He appreciated the accomplishments of people who had played a part in developing the United States.

BORGLUM'S CRAFT

Although critics judged Borglum's work as just "good," the American public liked the realistic action his monuments, paintings, and statues portrayed.

In 1915 Borglum was commissioned by the United Daughters of the Confederacy to sculpt a massive commemoration of the Civil War's Confederate army at Stone Mountain. Little work was completed during World War I, which spanned 1914–1918, but Borglum did begin a chisel outline of General Robert E. Lee. Borglum's personal boldness had become apparent when he undertook the immense project of carving Stone Mountain. By 1924 Borglum was involved in escalating conflicts of artistic control with Hollins N. Randolph, president of the Stone Mountain Monumental Association. As a result, the passionate, take-charge, energetic Borglum was fired from the project on February 5, 1925.

Before Borglum left, he destroyed the studio models of the sculpture so they could not be copied by another artist. This act outraged members of the association, who felt the models were their property. The local sheriff and a posse, armed with an arrest warrant, pursued Borglum to the state line. In anticipation of someday returning to Georgia, Borglum had even rebuilt the model of Stone Mountain in a Raleigh, North Carolina, studio. However, because of the anger that Borglum had created, he was never able to return to the Stone Mountain project, which disturbed him greatly. The pain caused by the Stone Mountain controversy eased slightly because Borglum (now with a tarnished reputation) was ready to tackle a new project.

SEARCHING THE BLACK HILLS

On that first trip in September 1924, Borglum was accompanied by his twelve-year-old son, Lincoln, and Major Jesse Tucker, his primary assistant at Stone Mountain. Along with their guides and several prominent South Dakotans, the three visitors spent several days scouting a site for the proposed monument. Since there were few roads, they covered the rough terrain by horseback and by hiking. Borglum concluded that the needles were unsuitable: They were badly weathered, consisted of irregular rock, and were proportionately wrong for carving.

However, Borglum did find the Harney mountain range to be a "veritable garden of the gods."[13] The deep canyons, caves, and coarse volcanic rock formations known as pegmatites provided a place for carving that was inaccessible to vandals. Having rejected the needles as inappropriate, Borglum would return to the Black Hills a year later to search for a more sound site for a massive monument.

A PROPOSED SKETCH

Shortly after his 1924 visit, Borglum submitted a sketch to Doane Robinson outlining his concept for a Black Hills memorial. The proposal showed separate standing figures of Washington and Lincoln carved on natural spires in the needles area. The statues were to be about two-hundred-feet tall.

Borglum also added that Theodore Roosevelt, General George A. Custer, and others would be part of the design. The delighted Robinson replied,

> I feel that the Washington and Lincoln busts should form the complete preliminary scheme. . . . There will be a dignity and grandeur about these two figures standing on top of the world which, it seems to me, would be minimized by an extension.[14]

Since the Harney mountain range was situated in a national forest and in a state park, both federal and state laws had to be passed authorizing any carving. The South Dakota legislature voted to permit carving in the Black Hills on March 5, 1925; however, it took a full year for the federal government to approve the project. Congressman William Williamson, who would be associated with the project until the monument was completed, drafted the federal bills that would authorize work in the national forest.

FINDING A MOUNTAIN

While awaiting federal approval, Borglum returned to South Dakota in August 1925 with his sketched plan to search for the right mountain on which to carve these two figures. Three important aspects of the project had to be decided: One was the site, the second was the subject matter to be carved, and the third was the method of financing the work. Again Borglum's son accompanied him on the search for the site. State forester Theodore Shoemaker of Keystone, South Dakota, was Borglum's chief guide. Shoemaker guided the group through almost every rocky upthrust of the Harney range. They inspected many cliffs and outcroppings, but Shoemaker had saved his personal favorite for last: the massive gray peak known as Mount Rushmore. As Lincoln Borglum recalls,

> This was the monolith my father had been searching for: a gigantic mountain of solid granite, towering above the

surrounding peaks and well separated from them. Most important, the major face of the rock was to the south-east, an aspect essential for maximum sunlight during the daytime hours. As he [Gutzon] talked in that positive, mesmerizing way of his, I began to see in the great peak the colossal mountain sculpture he could create here.[15]

Before finalizing his decision to use Mount Rushmore, Borglum and his troop camped at the bottom of the mountain and studied its southern face, its crevices and texture, and its size. Mount Rushmore towered six thousand feet above sea level. Its peak of solid granite was one-thousand-feet long and four-hundred-feet high. The best way to learn more about the mountain was to climb it.

The climbing group included Borglum, Lincoln, and other members of the search party. Reaching the top of the four-hundred-foot cliff, the climbers could see five thousand square

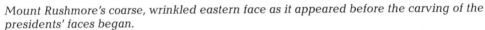

Mount Rushmore's coarse, wrinkled eastern face as it appeared before the carving of the presidents' faces began.

miles of mountains and plains stretching across western South Dakota into Nebraska, Wyoming, and beyond. Two more days were spent photographing the mountain for its illumination and shape. Samples of the stone were also removed for closer examination.

An Awesome Assignment

Borglum later recorded his emotions when he first saw the view from Rushmore's crest:

> I was conscious we were in another world . . . and there a new thought seized me—a thought that was to redirect me and dominate all my carving—the scale of that mountain peak!

> We looked out over a horizon level and beaten like the rim of a great cartwheel 2,000 feet below. We had reached upward toward the heavenly bodies . . . and it came over me in an almost terrifying manner that I had never sensed what I was planning. Plans must change. The vastness I saw here demanded it.[16]

Borglum had found the site for his carved memorial. He had chosen carefully and exuded confidence in his abilities, but he was unsure of what might be discovered when actual carving began. After all, much might be hidden in the granite cliff. Its face was like an aged elephant's hide—rough, cracked, wrinkled, and showing obvious blemishes—the result of millions of years of weathering and erosion. Nonetheless, Borglum did not believe the imperfections were deep enough to make the granite unusable.

It took Borglum four days to convince Senator Norbeck that this had to be the mountain. Norbeck was inclined to choose a mountain closer and more accessible to a populated area. The nearest existing road to Rushmore was a mile and a half away and meandered through jagged wilderness. Among other things, Norbeck worried about the cost of building roads into such a remote area.

Dedicating the Mountain

On October 1, 1925, Borglum staged the first of six celebrations at Mount Rushmore. Among the speakers at the mountain's

NAMING A MOUNTAIN

In his book *Mount Rushmore: The Story Behind the Scenery*, Lincoln Borglum tells how the huge granite cliff that was to become a memorial to four presidents and democracy was named.

Charles Rushmore had a mountain named after him by an impulsive Black Hills guide.

Until 1885 it [Mount Rushmore] didn't even have a name. That year a New York attorney, Charles E. Rushmore, hired to do some title investigation in the Black Hills, was looking over the country on horseback and, curious about the tall peak, asked his prospector-guide about it. The rough miner, given a chance to gently rib his eastern companion, replied (so the story goes), "Hell, it never *had* a name, but from now on we'll call the damn thing Rushmore." The name stuck, but until the day it was selected as the site for the huge memorial my father was to carve, there weren't many who cared what the mountain was called, and it wasn't until 1930, when the work on the mountain was already in progress, that the name was officially recognized. (Charles Rushmore was later to become one of the earliest contributors to the memorial, with a gift of $5,000.)

dedication were Robinson, Norbeck, and Borglum. Three thousand people struggled over the rough terrain to attend the historic event. A pine platform was erected a quarter of a mile southeast of Rushmore.

The pageantry included four eighteen-by-twenty-four-foot hand-stitched flags. The flags were ceremoniously raised by actors dressed in French, Spanish, and English costumes. A Sioux Indian dressed in full native attire was also present. These figures represented the former historic owners of the lands that surrounded Mount Rushmore. A thirty-piece band, Indian dances, speeches, and a meal consisting of sandwiches of barbecued elk and beef completed the day's activities. Borglum told the audience,

I confess I have never been free of fear and anxiety over the outcome of every phase of the undertaking, and quite apart from the enormous physical and nervous strain applied to the craftsmanship and the mechanism, there is the . . . hope that so great a mass can be made a tremendous emotional creation.[17]

CHOOSING THE SUBJECT MATTER

The next step was to choose the subject matter to be carved. Robinson's initial suggestion of heroes of western history did not suit Borglum. Borglum felt that this theme was too regional and nationally insignificant, and Robinson agreed with the persuasive

At the October 1, 1925, mountain dedication, Senator Peter Norbeck and Gutzon Borglum posed on the mountaintop with two actors dressed to represent former owners of surrounding lands.

sculptor. Borglum's monument, located in the heartland of the nation, would be more encompassing of American history.

Borglum insisted that the memorial display nobility and symbolize the founding, growth, preservation, and development of the nation. The basic ideal of American government—democracy—would be represented by those people selected. The sculptor chose four presidents to carry out this theme.

George Washington would be the dominant figure. As first president of the United States, he represented America's independence, the Constitution, and liberty.

NATIONAL HEARTBEATS

Gutzon Borglum, in his fondness for the United States and his proud patriotism, voiced his justifications for the enormous project. Lincoln Borglum, in his book *Mount Rushmore: The Story Behind the Scenery*, excerpts his father's writings.

A monument's dimensions should be determined by the importance to civilization of the events commemorated. We are not here trying to carve an epic, portray a moonlight scene, or write a sonnet; neither are we dealing with mystery or tragedy, but rather the constructive and the dramatic moments or crises in our amazing history. We are cool-headedly, clear-mindedly setting down a few crucial, epochal [memorable] facts regarding the accomplishments of the Old World radicals who shook the shackles of oppression from their light feet and fled despotism [tyranny] to people a continent; who built an empire and rewrote the philosophy of freedom and compelled the world to accept its wiser, happier forms of government.

We believe the dimensions of national heartbeats are greater than village impulses, greater than city demands, greater than state dreams or ambitions. Therefore, we believe a nation's memorial should, like Washington, Jefferson, Lincoln, and Roosevelt, have a serenity, a nobility, a power that reflects the gods who inspired them and suggests the gods they have become.

Thomas Jefferson was chosen for two reasons: He authored the Declaration of Independence, and he was also president when the United States bought the Louisiana Territory from France in 1803 at a cost of about three cents an acre—a bargain that doubled the country's land mass. South Dakota was one of the states eventually carved from that territory.

The third choice, Abraham Lincoln, was a favorite of Borglum's. He admired Lincoln's strength in holding the country together during the Civil War as well as his belief in freedom for all Americans.

Theodore Roosevelt, the fourth choice, met with some objections at first. Roosevelt had been dead only six years, and opponents felt the value of his contributions to America were too shallow. But Borglum wanted his sculpture to include "nation builders." He felt that Roosevelt's participation in linking the Atlantic and Pacific Oceans by building the Panama Canal, and thus easing commerce between America's east and west coasts, qualified him for inclusion in this select group. In Borglum's opinion, the feat of building the Panama Canal completed the national expansion of the United States.

With the site and figures to be carved decided upon, financing remained to be worked out. It was clear that the state government could not cover the costs alone. Lots of money would be needed, and finding it would prove to be a job that Borglum could not do by himself.

Finances: A Problem
from the Start

After the memorial's dedication, the Black Hills area was bursting with excitement, publicity, and optimism. The Rapid City *Daily Journal* editorialized the meaning of the memorial and its potential importance:

> Never in its history has the city been so profoundly moved as it has been in connection with the carving of the memorial on Rushmore. Just the idea has given us a better perspective upon our national ideals, our national history and our world wide mission. It has turned our minds from the small things of today and given us a vision of the great things of the past and of the future.[18]

As it turned out, almost two years passed before carving on the mountain even started. Most of that time was spent obtaining financing for the project.

Raising Funds

Borglum had been optimistic that he could easily find big contributors for building the memorial. Estimating the total cost at between four hundred thousand and eight hundred thousand dollars, Borglum insisted that some rich individual could be persuaded to finance at least one carved figure or perhaps even the entire memorial.

From the outset, however, Borglum made serious mistakes regarding funds. For example, he led many people to believe that the entire project could be privately funded. "You're not asked to spend a dollar on the project,"[19] he told Rapid City residents. Many times Borglum assured Robinson and Norbeck that he had talked with friends who knew two men who would provide the money for carving Washington and Jefferson. However, these benefactors never came forward.

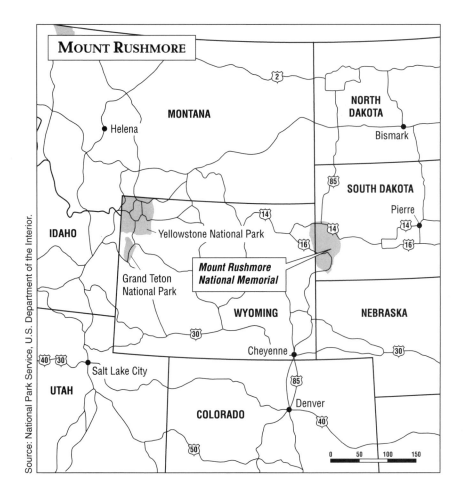

As the project's expense and complexity became clear, the Mount Harney Memorial Association was formed in 1925 to help oversee the work. It was composed of South Dakota businessmen and boosters. The association's job was to control the finances and supervise the carving. Borglum formed a cordial working relationship with members of the Mount Harney commission—at least in the beginning. The sculptor aggressively and persistently pushed forward, using his own money for travel and speaking engagements.

PROMOTERS

The strongest promoters—Borglum, Robinson, and Norbeck—did their part in trying to obtain funding. During 1926 Borglum constructed the first model of the monument in his San Antonio,

Gutzon Borglum chisels at an early model that shows the original positions of three presidents. The model would be altered nine times due to cracks and uncarvable rock.

Texas, studio. He photographed the model and showed the designs during his many fund-raising speeches in major cities around the country. Although this activity generated much publicity, little money came in.

Robinson flooded the postal system with letters to distinguished, wealthy Americans. He suggested that anyone wishing to finance one of the Rushmore figures would not only be performing "a great patriotic service" but would also be "perpetuating his own name and fame to the centuries."[20] However, Robinson found no one willing to make such a contribution.

Senator Norbeck attempted to use his influence to convince South Dakota's legislature to accept responsibility for two items. One was to build a decent road to the memorial, and the second was to earmark ten thousand dollars for the Rushmore carving itself. But the state governor, Carl Gunderson, who opposed the project, saw to it that the legislature took no action on appropriating funds for the project.

FOOLHARDY BEHAVIOR

Even though no money was available to pay Borglum's expenses and he had no commitments, contract, or even promises, he boldly pushed on with the project. In August 1926 Borglum moved his family into a primitive cabin in Keystone, South Dakota. For three weeks Borglum and Jesse Tucker marked the rugged surface of Mount Rushmore in preparation for carving.

Borglum continued to be upbeat about funding. He even requested the building of a road to the site and money for a comprehensive study of the mountain. The sculptor told South Dakota supporters that he knew "swarms of malefactors [law breakers] of great wealth [who would] gladly and readily contribute conscience money to popular public memorials."[21] Borglum tried to downplay how much the project would cost and even made the rash statement that he did not want to be paid for his labors, only his expenses.

A ray of hope appeared in the November 1926 elections when Governor Gunderson, who still opposed construction of the monument, was defeated by William J. Bulow, who mildly favored the project. Also, another important Rushmore booster arrived on the scene at this time. He was Rapid City businessman John Boland. In 1927 Boland took charge of soliciting substantial donations from Black Hills business owners, especially those in Rapid City. Although Boland and Borglum were different in temperament, their relationship was cordial—at first.

HOPES AND PLANS

In the beginning of 1927, with little money coming in, the Mount Rushmore project was nearly abandoned. Borglum reasoned that no money was forthcoming from his wealthy friends because South Dakota had shown indifference by not contributing funds to the project.

Borglum's problems were made worse by the fact that he was under a great strain from creditors and work contracts. He was overdue for payments on his studios in Raleigh, North Carolina, and in San Antonio, Texas. Furthermore, Borglum had also absorbed all of his Rushmore promotional expenses. To help repay these debts, Borglum drove himself to take on other sculptural commissions, while still promoting Rushmore.

KILL THE PROJECT!

When financing for the monument faltered, Rushmore's opponents invited people to contribute belittling remarks that would discredit Borglum. Critic John Tjaden from the University of South Dakota wrote the following poem, which was published in several of the state's newspapers and was reprinted in Rex Alan Smith's *The Carving of Mount Rushmore.*

> When God made our matchless playground,
> He did not intend that man should
> even in his wildest ravings
> dare to come with hammer, chisel,
> block and tackle, pick and mallet,
> to profane His age-old record,
> to profane the face of Rushmore
> by his puny, pygmy scratches.
>
> Why should man presume to alter
> the Creator's masterpieces,
> wrought in everlasting granite,
> wrought by forces so titanic
> that no scientist can measure,
> that no human mind can master?
> And to think that man, presumptive,
> should deface and mutilate them!
>
> Men and women, 'tis your duty
> to lift up your earnest voices,
> to the end that all our people
> forthwith band themselves together
> to preserve from desecration
> finished products from God's workshop
> and placed by the Master-Artist
> in the playground of Dakota.

Fund-raising for the Rushmore project was virtually at a standstill, and Borglum searched for unique ways to obtain money. The federal government had appropriated millions of dollars for statues, monuments, and memorials from its very beginning in 1789, and Borglum hoped it would help with money for Rushmore.

One financing idea was for the government to mint fifty-cent coins that would be sold for one dollar each. Borglum knew from past experience that this plan would not be accepted, but he hoped that rejection of one idea might make a second suggestion more agreeable. This second option was to request a direct appropriation from the government. The scheme eventually worked, although it required several years of courting the right political leaders in Washington. It would take some luck for the Mount Rushmore project to stay on track.

ANOTHER STROKE OF LUCK

During the summer of 1927 the state of South Dakota basked in good fortune. Advisers to President Calvin Coolidge had suggested that he spend his summer somewhere in the Midwest in order to build support among farmers for his reelection. He chose the Black Hills for his three-month respite.

After the announcement of Coolidge's upcoming summer visit, Boland got busy arranging for enough funds to allow construction to begin on Mount Rushmore. He solicited five thousand dollars from each of the four railroads serving the state and from the Homestake Mining Company. New York attorney Charles E. Rushmore, for whom the mountain had been named, also donated five thousand dollars. Other donations from the First National Bank, Rapid City firms, and individuals brought the total to over fifty-four thousand dollars.

In addition, Boland and the Mount Harney Memorial Association started a fund drive in South Dakota's schools. The pennies and nickels collected from the children were intended to show the world how much the monument meant to residents of South Dakota.

With the last donations in place, the association could now draw up contracts for Borglum and Tucker. On March 1, 1927, Borglum signed a formal contract, in which he agreed to forego a salary. Instead, he was to be paid 25 percent of all the money spent on labor, supplies, and machinery, but the total paid to him was not to exceed $87,500. Including that amount, the planners estimated the cost of the project to be a maximum of $437,500. Borglum was also given "full, final and complete freedom and authority" for the monument's "artistic excellence."[22]

Lincoln Borglum describes his father's expected responsibilities:

> He [Gutzon] was, of course, to plan the design and then work out the engineering problems and techniques. There were no guidelines or precedents on mountain carving, beyond those he himself had established at Stone Mountain, and no skilled carvers available. He must train local miners to be assistant sculptors. These challenges may have overwhelmed a lesser man, but my father was, after all, an artist—a man with a special destiny and a larger vision.[23]

Borglum's assistant, Tucker, was promised ten thousand dollars per year. Because Borglum was working on other commissions, he depended on Tucker to see to the day-to-day operations at Rushmore. Tucker was the only other man in the world with any practical knowledge of mountain carving and in using dynamite for stone removal.

To attract more interest nationwide, Borglum submitted illustrations of his carved model of Washington, Jefferson, and Lincoln to the March 1927 issue of *Popular Mechanics* magazine. The pictures clarified his plan to tell the nation's story on a mountain. Borglum also described his desire to carve in fourteen-foot-high letters "a huge tablet bearing the great dates in the history of the United States and simple statements of the significance of each."[24] At this time, Borglum planned to carve the tablet on the mountain's west wall, which would not interfere with the sculpture on the east wall.

THE FIRST PREPARATIONS

Borglum was determined to take advantage of the publicity that would result from the president's sojourn in South Dakota. He and Tucker immediately hired sixteen men. Construction of a building to house a huge diesel engine began in Keystone, three miles away. The two-hundred-horsepower engine would generate electricity to operate three air compressors at the base of the mountain.

Strapped in bosun's seats, Borglum (bottom), his assistant, Jesse Tucker (middle), and an unidentified crew member inspect the steep face of the mountain.

Compressors, jackhammers, and other equipment were ordered. By July 10 the first machinery was unloaded at the site. Workers hacked a path through the thick forest for power lines and forged a rough road for mule wagons to use in hauling the heavy equipment. The air compressors would push air through a three-inch air line that traveled all the way to the top of the mountain—some fourteen hundred feet. This compressed air would power the drills.

The sixteen workmen sweated and labored for a month, lugging heavy equipment and supplies. Crude buildings were constructed on the mountaintop. An old log cabin at the base of the mountain was renovated for use as a temporary studio for Borglum. The men also dug a well for drinking water, dammed a stream to supply water for cooling the compressors, and constructed a cookhouse.

All of these preparations were to be completed by August 10, the date Borglum had chosen for the celebration that would accompany the first drilling. Final and frantic tests were made on compressors and air pipes. Elaborate plans for a ceremony, with President Coolidge participating, were put into action. The monument desperately needed publicity, and this opportunity to include the president of the United States in the celebration was extraordinary.

WELCOMING PRESIDENT COOLIDGE

The president; his wife, Grace; a large party of aides; Secret Service agents; and newspaper reporters arrived in South Dakota on June 15, 1927. The memorial's backers wanted to make the most of the president's visit by generating positive publicity. Steps were taken to ensure that President Coolidge would be the recipient of midwestern hospitality.

Coolidge was staying at the Game Lodge in Custer State Park. Hanging Squaw Creek, the clear stream running past the lodge, was renamed Grace Coolidge Creek. Because the president was an avid fisherman, townspeople wanted to make sure fish would be caught during his stay. To accomplish this, a half-mile section of the creek was blocked off with underwater wire-netting fish fences and stocked with prize trout. Soon after his arrival, the president unpacked his fly rod and checked out the creek. A quick couple of casts yielded instant catches. He told reporters on the bank that he was "either the best fisherman alive or the luckiest."[25]

PRESIDENT COOLIDGE ATTENDS THE CEREMONY

Borglum did everything he could to make the president and his party feel welcome. On the morning of August 10, the day chosen for the first drilling, Borglum hired a local stunt pilot to fly him in an open cockpit biplane over the Game Lodge. As they flew in low, Borglum dropped a large wreath of wildflowers into the yard for Grace Coolidge, who had come out to wave when she heard the airplane noise.

Next, limousines escorted the presidential party to the work site. The president rode a horse up a steep embankment to the speaker's platform, which had been set up on Doane Mountain. Dressed in a traditional three-piece suit, the president had added cowboy boots and a ten-gallon hat to his wardrobe for the occasion.

In his dry New England manner, Coolidge delivered a short speech to the crowd of seventeen hundred picnickers:

> We have come here to dedicate a cornerstone that was laid by the hand of the Almighty. . . . The people of the future will see history and art combined to portray the spirit of patriotism. . . . This memorial will be another national shrine to which future generations will repair [go] to declare their continuing allegiance to independence, to self government, to freedom and to economic justice. [South

At the August 10, 1927, formal dedication ceremony, President Calvin Coolidge, dressed in cowboy boots, removed his ten-gallon hat while delivering a short speech.

Dakotans deserve] the sympathy and support of private beneficence [financial gifts] and the national government. . . . Money spent for such a purpose is certain of adequate returns in the nature of increased public welfare.[26]

BORGLUM STAGES THE FIRST DRILLING

After his speech, Coolidge handed a set of steel drills to Borglum. Using this opportune moment to solidify Coolidge's support, Borglum said to the president, "As the first president who has taken part, please write the inscription to go on that mountain. We want your connection known in some other way than by your presence. I want the name of Coolidge on that mountain."[27]

Next, the crowd watched as Borglum and Tucker left the platform stage and went to the Rushmore cliff to climb the wooden steps to the mountaintop. Holding their breath, they saw Borglum being lowered in a leather-strapped swing, known as a bosun's seat, attached to a steel cable. From that distance, it looked as though Tucker was lowering the fearless Borglum by a thread.

Suddenly the crowd heard the staccato noise from a jackhammer. This jarring sound heralded the first drilled holes for Washington's forehead. Looking like a fly on a wall, Borglum was raised and lowered to six different locations on Rushmore's mountain face. When he returned to the stage, Borglum ceremoniously gave drill bits in turn to President Coolidge, Senator Norbeck, and Doane Robinson.

At the dedication, Borglum prepares to drill the first holes for Washington's forehead.

After the ceremony Robinson thanked Coolidge for his participation. The president said, "I made the address very brief and explicit for I thought you might want to print it to help you get the money."[28]

President Coolidge's three-month visit to the Black Hills gave the monument a tremendous nationwide boost, and contributions started to come in. Coolidge's support of the project was also instrumental in establishing Mount Rushmore as a national memorial and in securing funds from the U.S. government.

MORE PREPARATIONS

After the ceremonial first drilling, two months were spent with necessary preparations before actual work could begin. Construction at the base of the mountain included a bunkhouse for the workmen, a blacksmith's shop, tool sheds, and a cableway. On the mountaintop, walkways connected a myriad of buildings: a repair shop, sheds, winch houses, an office, and a workers' shelter. Hand-operated winches were set up and fastened to the mountaintop with steel pins. These winches controlled the steel cables used to lower workmen over the mountainside.

Borglum's model of the four heads arrived from his San Antonio office, but not without incident. While transporting the model to the Black Hills in his automobile, Lincoln Borglum fell asleep at the wheel, went off the road, and overturned the car. Luckily, Borglum's son was not injured and the presidents' faces were not damaged. Only the base of the model, which portrayed the mountain, and Borglum's car were in need of repair. Borglum took the news of the accident calmly, saying only that it was "easier to repair a broken mountain than a broken boy."[29]

TEENAGE MISHAP

In his book *My Father's Mountain: Mt. Rushmore National Memorial and How It Was Carved,* Lincoln Borglum describes the harrowing task of moving his father's model of the Rushmore heads from San Antonio, Texas, to South Dakota's Black Hills.

By the time I was in high school, my father had his ambitious carving underway—despite a small setback from myself. He had completed his first design for the mountain in his San Antonio studio, and instructed me to put it in the back of the car and bring it to the Black Hills during my summer vacation. Unfortunately, I fell asleep at the wheel, rolled the car in a ditch and broke the model. The four heads came through intact, but my father had to make major repairs on the base. It also took three days and $100 to fix his automobile, which didn't contribute any to his disposition. After that, my contributions to the mountain were of a more constructive nature.

BORGLUM'S ERRATIC PERSONALITY

Borglum displayed his volatile temperament during this early stage of work. He criticized Robinson and the Mount Harney Memorial Association for inefficient work, poor construction, and petty economies. The main clash was over Borglum's need for a studio, which had not been included in the request for equipment. The usually mild and even-tempered Robinson released a stinging reply to Borglum's complaints: "I am not worth a damn at divining [guessing] what a man has in the back of his head and does not reveal. . . . You think it is artistic temperament, but to me it seems childishness, pettiness, unworthy of a man of your great gifts."[30] This early confrontation put a strain on their relationship.

A second argument arose over the quality of paper that Robinson had chosen for printing copies of Coolidge's Mount Rushmore speech. The speech was to be included with letters appealing for funds. The ordinary paper on which the speech was printed looked cheap to Borglum, and he was angered by this meager economy. Luckily, when Borglum scolded Robinson about this matter, Norbeck—who sometimes played the role of a referee—was present. Norbeck's comment to the two men headed off a serious quarrel: "Doane, you should have printed the speech on better paper; and Gutzon, you shouldn't have said a damn thing about it."[31]

DRILLING BEGINS

During 1927 a daily report was kept of activities and progress. An entry dated October 4 states, "Today we started the actual drilling on Rushmore. Several holes were drilled and equipment tried out."[32] Soon the mountain buzzed with noise and activity, and the Rushmore memorial showed signs of the shrine it would become. Although the initial challenges had been overcome, more would soon surface.

Suspended from cables, drillers balance and brace themselves as they become accustomed to handling jackhammers and air hoses on the mountain face.

A SMALL BEGINNING

Borglum was constantly challenged by what lay beneath the surface of the mountain. Before the carving could begin, it was important to decide on the approximate location of each head on the face of the cliff and how each would fit, given the cracks that were present in the mountain. Borglum used his plaster model for reference, but he changed the model nine times before the monument was completed.

Borglum chose to ignore a professional geologist's warnings about the deep-angled cracks on the mountain's surface. Consequently, many of the sculptor's calculations resulted in expensive mistakes. Besides the challenges posed by the mountain's surface, Borglum had to deal with other problems, such as transferring measurements onto the cliff face, transporting supplies to the job, and finding fearless workers.

Doing It the Hard Way

Most sculptors would have stripped the entire mountain face free of blemishes before starting the actual carving, but Borglum chose to rough out one head at a time. He did not position the next head until he could see how it would blend with the work already done and the natural formations of the surrounding mountain. As Borglum explains,

> The one successful way to proceed . . . is to adapt the sculp-
> tured forms to the existing stone formation, and *not* to con-
> vert the mountain into an architectural form and then
> transform the sculpture to fit it. Sculptured work on a
> mountain must *belong* to the mountain as a natural part of
> it; otherwise it becomes a hideous mechanical application.[33]

The Beginning

Eager to embark on this gigantic project, Borglum chose the initial placement for the figures on the massive granite mountainside. His son, Lincoln, recounts the difficulties they encountered with Rushmore:

Standing a long distance away, Borglum examines progress on his monumental dream.

The biggest construction problem was that the composition of the work could not be predetermined. Mt. Rushmore turned out to be a constant struggle between composition and finding solid stone for each of the four heads.

The mountain has four main fissures cutting through it at an angle of about 45 degrees and about 70 feet apart. They do not follow straight planes of cleavage [splitting], so the definite location of any of the heads could not be determined until all have been completely roughed out. Each was shifted several times.[34]

Borglum decided to make Washington the dominant figure of the monument. He situated Washington's head on the highest and most prominent part of the cliff.

Once Washington's location had been determined, the next task was to translate the measurements of the model to those of the actual carving. At the Stone Mountain memorial in Georgia, Borglum used a powerful projecting lamp to cast his model sketches onto the face of the mountain at night. Although the projections were distorted, he had his workmen outline the figures with paint. This technique had worked for flat figures, but it could not be used for rounded ones like on Rushmore. Moreover, due to the unevenness of the mountain, the projection of the images would be like casting a picture on the side of a sack of potatoes.

DEVELOPING A POINTING MACHINE

Borglum devised a revolutionary way to transfer his model's dimensions to the mountain. He constructed two sizes of pointing machines, one size for each of the model heads and a proportionately larger one for each of the actual heads. His model was sized so that one inch on the model was equal to twelve inches on the mountain. The center of the top of each head was considered the master point, from which everything was measured.

Beginning with the Washington model, Borglum mounted an upright metal rod at the top center of the head. A flat protractor plate, marked off in degrees from zero to one hundred and eighty, was attached at the base of the rod. A horizontal

BORGLUM'S POINTING MACHINE

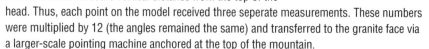

Borglum invented a pointing machine to transfer dimensions from his plaster models to the face of the mountain. The models were sized to a ratio of 1:12—one inch on the model would equal one foot on the mountain. A metal shaft (1) was placed upright at the center of the model's head. Attached at the base of the shaft was a protractor plate (2), marked in degrees, and a horizontal ruled bar (3) that pivoted to measure the angle from the axis. A weighted plumb line (4) hung from the bar; it slid back and forth to measure the distance from the central head point, and raised and lowered to measure vertical distance from the top of the head. Thus, each point on the model received three seperate measurements. These numbers were multiplied by 12 (the angles remained the same) and transferred to the granite face via a larger-scale pointing machine anchored at the top of the mountain.

Source: National Park Service, U.S. Department of the Interior.

ruled bar extended from the center point of the plate. Its pivoting movement allowed Borglum to measure angles. A weighted line, called a plumb bob, hung from the bar. It slid back and forth to measure horizontal distance from the central head point. The plumb line also moved up and down for vertical measurements from the top of the head.

These horizontal and vertical measurements were then multiplied by twelve and transferred to the mountain. The angle measurements remained the same. The eyes, nose, cheekbones, and lips had three separate measurements: a horizontal, a vertical, and an angle.

For example, a pointing machine followed these steps when transferring the dimension for the 60-inch face model. To transfer a nose measurement from the model to the mountain, the plumb bob was dropped on the model from the horizontal bar to the nose point. This resulted in three measurements: a horizontal bar measurement of 30 inches, a vertical plumb bob measurement of 40 inches, and an angle measurement of 90 degrees. Using both a swinging boom and a plumb bob on the mountain, these numbers translated to a horizontal measurement of 360 inches (30 feet), a vertical measurement of 480 inches (40 feet), and an angle measurement remaining at 90 degrees. This spot was then marked with paint on the mountain designating the nose point. The system of using the pointing machines on the model and mountain proved so effective that it was used throughout Rushmore's construction.

Men trained to be pointers held important positions in the work crew. The pointer was responsible for all measurements and approved all drilling and blasting. It was the pointer's job to mark the mountain with painted instructions telling how deep to drill at any given point. These marks then guided the drillers.

GETTING SUPPLIES AND MEN TO THE JOB

Dynamite sticks, drill bits (sized in length from a few inches to twenty feet), and other supplies had to be transported to the mountaintop. Four hundred drill bits were used on peak workdays, and a blacksmith stationed at the base of the mountain kept busy sharpening bits that had been dulled by use.

A thirteen-hundred-foot-long cableway was built to carry materials up the mountain. The cableway consisted of a steel mining bucket on a trolley. It could only hold five hundred

A pointer, carrying a can of paint, marks the mountain face with depth instructions for the drillers and blasters. These orders told the workers how much stone needed to be removed.

pounds and was considered unsafe for the men to ride. Borglum, however, disregarding his own safety, often rode up and down the mountain in the bucket.

The workers had to reach the mountaintop by climbing a newly built stairway that consisted of 760 steps. This hike was equivalent to climbing the stairs of a forty-story building. Each morning the men arrived at the mountaintop breathless and exhausted. It would be nine years before the aerial tramway was upgraded to transport workmen to the faces.

Eight hand-cranked winches were enclosed in buildings on the mountaintop. After the long climb, winch men raised and lowered drillers and blasters in bosun's seats to their positions on the mountain face.

Once the placement of Washington's head had been determined and the pointing and carving procedures had been laid out, Borglum transferred the supervision of the work to his assistant, Major Tucker. Borglum then departed for his San Antonio studio to work on other assignments. Following Borglum's instructions, Tucker used the pointing machine to first rough out the Washington head. Next he "peeled off," or blasted, the surface until he reached sound carving stone. Heavy blasting, the first stage of carving, was done by drillers in bosun's seats.

THE JOB OF A DRILLER

Drillers, some of whom had been trained as miners, were accustomed to working on solid ground; now they had to become accustomed to dangling over a mountainside from a three-eighths-inch-thick cable that was attached to a winch on top of the mountain. In addition to hanging five hundred feet above the ground, the drillers had to cope with maneuvering a jackhammer. This air-driven machine weighed from twenty to sixty pounds and was attached to one side of the seat with a hard-to-manage air hose.

Since the drillers could neither see the winch house nor its operator, they had to signal a callboy, who was positioned in a harness on the lip of the cliff and could see both the driller and the winch operator, when they wanted to be moved to another spot on the mountain. Each cabled harness had a number corresponding to its winch. Using a microphone attached to a loudspeaker in the winch house, the callboy would yell "six up" or "six down," meaning raise or lower winch number six. Winch men responded by hand-winding the cable.

The bosun's seats used by drillers and blasters were developed by Borglum and had been used experimentally at Stone Mountain. A wide belt encircled the wearer's waist and attached to a strap that passed between his legs, holding him safely in place. Workers were assured that it was impossible to fall out of the seat, even if he should lose consciousness. But to a worker looking down at Rushmore's buildings, which appeared to be the size of dollhouses, that assurance failed to make the job any less scary. As a Rushmore driller recalls,

They gave me my jackhammer and they gave me my drills, and I went down over that mountain and stayed 'til noon. Then I went back and stayed 'til night. But, God! It scared me! No two ways about it. But I did that for three or four days and, no foolin', I'd wake up in the night and grab that old bed and hang on for all I was worth, thinkin' I was fallin' off that mountain. Somehow you never had any faith in that cable, and you could look down and see just where you'd fall to, and it looked so damned far! So I told Mr. Denison, "God! I just can't do that! I can't sleep at night and I'm scared to death hangin' out there on that dinky cable." So he gave me a different job and I stayed at Rushmore until it was finished.[35]

Rushmore drillers learned special techniques, such as how to lean back in their seats, "walk" up and down at the same rate at which the operator was using the cable, handle their jack-hammers in awkward positions, and hold drill bits between their

Working in a hoist house on the mountaintop, operators responding to a callboy's instructions raise and lower drillers and blasters in bosun's seats by hand cranking the cables on the winches.

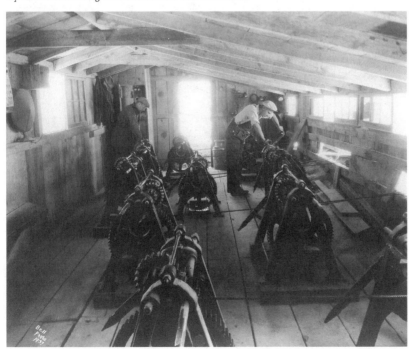

CLOSE TO HEAVEN

Gutzon Borglum admitted it was dangerous for men to work at such tremendous heights. In *Mount Rushmore: The Story Behind the Scenery*, Lincoln Borglum quotes his father regarding the attitude of the workmen on the cliff.

> We needed and were developing in ourselves much courage, for much as we whistled over our job, we . . . were constantly aware of the proximity of . . . a very real graveyard all about us. Were we afraid? Certainly, we were afraid, every mother's son of us, but I believe we enjoyed even that. [We] very soon became used to [our] situation between heaven and death and we lost thought of the hazard.

Pride in the historic venture overcame fear as men swung out over Washington's facial features.

feet to prevent the bits from bouncing over the stone as they started a new hole. During October 1929 the work of five or six drill operators kept clouds of granite dust constantly floating in the mountain air.

Getting Started

Mount Rushmore's ancient surface was badly fractured and too spongy for carving. Borglum hoped to place the heads so that a fissure, or crack, would not be at a delicate spot of the face, such as the nose or chin. Facial features with splits in them would weather off in a few hundred or a few thousand years. Because so much rock had to be blasted away before solid granite was reached, Washington's chin is thirty feet back from the original surface of the mountain.

Before actual carving of a figure could begin, tons of unusable rock had to be removed to reach a suitable surface. At first jackhammers were used to drill the rock away, but this was slow and therefore expensive. Within three weeks Borglum decided to use dynamite to blast off the outer rock to get rid of the blemishes. The October 25 entry in the daily report states, "The chief event of today was the trying of dynamite in blasting off rock."[36]

Borglum's experience at Stone Mountain had taught him that dynamite could be used efficiently and safely to remove large quantities of stone. Powder men, known as powder monkeys, prepared the dynamite charges, placed the explosives into drilled holes, and lit the fuses. While carving with dynamite, Borglum had learned "two considerations to be borne constantly in mind—split off just what you want to remove and no more, and second, under no conditions so charge your load as to injure the stone left in place."[37]

Quick Progress

As a result of the daily dynamite blasting, progress was soon evident on the mountain. The first step in the process of blasting required parallel holes to be drilled about six feet deep. About twenty holes, spaced eighteen inches apart, were drilled. Next, a powder monkey placed sticks of dynamite into the holes and then packed in damp sand. The sand absorbed some of the jarring effect of the blast, thus protecting the remaining stone.

Another row of holes was drilled about three feet above this row. Workers always moved upward so they would be out of

Beginning with the Washington figure, the mountain face would be blasted off to reach a usable surface. During dynamiting, canyons echoed and dust floated in the air as granite chunks plunged down the mountain.

danger from falling rocks in case of accidental discharge. The dynamite charges were wired together and blasting took place during the lunch break and at the end of the day when workers were safely on top of the mountain or had gone home. Twice a day the canyons echoed with great blasts as tons of granite toppled down the mountain.

The process was repeated until suitable stone was reached. As blasters came closer to a firm surface, they drilled the holes shallower and closer together and reduced the size of the explosive charges. In the latter stages of removing stone, only cap charges were used and were quite accurate—within one to three inches of the desired surface.

WASHINGTON'S FOREHEAD

As the dark-colored rough exterior was blasted away, a light-colored granite appeared. Workers had penetrated six feet from

DYNAMITE

Dynamite charges were prepared by workers known as powdermen in a shed at the top of the mountain. To avoid shattering any carving surfaces, many small charges—sixty or seventy in a single shot—were assembled. Author Rex Alan Smith details dynamite characteristics in *The Carving of Mount Rushmore.*

Charges are prepared by cutting sticks of dynamite into lengths as short as an inch or even shorter, depending on the delicacy of the shot, and carefully tying into each length an electric detonator cap. It is tedious work and must be done with great care. Cutting the sticks like this exposes the naked dynamite to the powdermen's touch, and there is something in the stuff that, if you are not wearing gloves, will seep through the pores of your hands and cause a dull, pounding ache at the base of the skull that is aptly called a "dynamite headache." The dynamite itself is not dangerous to work with unless it is old. In old dynamite the nitroglycerine tends to gather and crystallize until it becomes as treacherous as a rattlesnake. This is why Johnson and the other powdermen at Rushmore will never carry over unused dynamite from one season to the next. Fresh dynamite, however, can be dropped, stepped on, thrown, even burned, without exploding. It can be detonated only by a mighty shock, and that is the purpose of the caps.

Powdermen carefully prepare dynamite charges for the next blast.

These tiny copper cylinders, each attached to a pair of four-foot-long electric wires, are packed with an explosive so powerful that a cap detonated inside a steel barrel will blast bits of its copper jacket clear through the barrel's walls. Unlike the dynamite, moreover, the caps are touchy and do not forgive carelessness. The powderman who forgets that is likely to lose a finger, hand, eye, or his life.

the outer surface and twenty-five feet down from Washington's forehead to the eyes. Much progress had been made, but by December 7 the first portion of the money was gone. Furthermore, the weather was deteriorating. With the temperature in the area falling to twenty-two degrees below zero, operations ceased. At the time, Borglum noted in his journal, "Operations shut down because of severe cold and exhausted funds."[38]

With no additional funds forthcoming, activity on the mountain was suspended during the entire following year of 1928. During that year, Congress would be bombarded with pleas not to let the project perish.

GOVERNMENT COMES TO THE RESCUE

Borglum remained hopeful despite the lack of funds to continue his work on Rushmore. He believed his influential friends could convince congressional leaders to support the project with government funds. But for eighteen months, work on Mount Rushmore remained at a standstill.

THE RUSHMORE BATTLE MOVES TO WASHINGTON, D.C.

Early in 1928 the bill to provide more money for Rushmore faced several fierce opponents in Congress. It was the responsibility of members of South Dakota's delegation, particularly Senator Peter Norbeck and Representative William Williamson, to change the minds of their peers. Wooing his fellow senators, Norbeck finally got the bill passed in the Senate.

However, the bill progressed with agonizing slowness through the House of Representatives. The difficult task facing Representative Williamson was to convince a majority of the 435 members to support the bill. When the final bill was presented to both houses of Congress, Senator Louis Cramton of Michigan held out for several amendments, but in the end only one amendment was attached, providing that no charge ever be made for admission to the memorial. Robinson, Borglum, and Norbeck opposed the no-charge concept, but they had to accept it in order to get the bill passed. The policy of free public admission to the memorial

Representative William Williamson persuaded the majority in the House of Representatives to support a bill to provide money for the Rushmore project.

remains to this day, except for a fee for parking in the main lot.

With all the dissension in Washington, D.C., Borglum decided that he did not want the government involved in the project. He preferred private financing and even sent Norbeck a telegram saying that he did not want the government's $250,000 appropriation. As the exasperated Norbeck wrote to Robinson,

> He [Borglum] does not want the quarter of a million from Congress now. He wants to go to New York, London, Jerusalem, or Heaven to get millions. . . . He is quite certain that a million is more than a quarter of a million, but that is the only thing he is sure about.[39]

Norbeck wrote Borglum a firm but diplomatic reply: "You are wholly uninformed of actual conditions. . . . Our only chance to avoid absolute failure seems to be government appropriation. . . . We do not want to fizzle. . . . I know you are busy and those telegrams are written under strain."[40]

Borglum accepted Norbeck's reasoning but proposed a new design idea: "We would extend the development around the memorial into possibly very fine buildings . . . for the purpose of the historical records bearing directly upon the matters the memorial commemorates."[41] Thus, in addition to the four presidential heads and a giant entablature, or inscription, Borglum wanted to add buildings to display historical records. Eventually this would be referred to as the Hall of Records.

As it turned out, Congress adjourned before agreeing on the Rushmore bill and further action was postponed six months. This delay worried the Rushmore backers. Herbert Hoover had been elected president; unsure of his support, they wanted the bill passed before President Coolidge would leave office in March 1929. When Congress reassembled, Norbeck convinced Cramton to drop two of his amendments to the bill. Removing this stumbling block opened the doors for easy passage.

THE RUSHMORE MEMORIAL RECEIVES GOVERNMENT AID

On February 22, 1929, ten days before his presidency ended, President Coolidge signed Public Law #805, making Mount Rushmore a national memorial comprising four figures. The law authorized the president to appoint a twelve-member Mount Rushmore National Memorial Commission, which replaced the Mount Harney Memorial Association. The bill also authorized Coolidge to write a brief history of the United States, which would be carved on a huge entablature to be included as part of the monument. In addition, it provided $250,000 in federal funds that were to be matched, dollar for dollar, with funds obtained from private donations.

This photo, taken July 17, 1929, shows the original Mount Rushmore National Memorial Commission posing in front of the mountain. Borglum, wearing a hat, appears in the front row.

Borglum handpicked members for the new commission, which would be appointed by Coolidge before he left office. Chosen primarily on the basis of their wealth, Borglum saw these commissioners as potential contributors. As soon as the commission was formally sworn in, work on the mountain could begin again. The only problem now was Borglum himself.

BORGLUM IRRITATES OTHERS

A week after Hoover took office, Borglum brazenly prodded the new president to meet with the new Mount Rushmore commission:

> I take it for granted you have been too much absorbed in the initial work of what I expect to be one of the most productive administrations America has enjoyed in her existence to have come in contact with the new federal commission to take over the national memorial in South Dakota.[42]

Borglum's note annoyed Hoover, and the new president purposely delayed meeting with the commission until June 6, 1929. The delay irked the sculptor and resulted in a coolness between the two men. For the first time in thirty years Borglum would not have friendly access to the White House.

Borglum had many friends in Congress and had always counted on them to speak to the president on his behalf. In addition, he often went to Washington and met with other members of Congress without first conferring with Norbeck. This ruffled Norbeck, of course, who wrote to Robinson,

> My own opinion is that the new commission will have to be more firm with Borglum than we have been. His enthusiasm knows no bounds and his originality is marvelous. His enthusiasm is something that is needed in the undertaking, but his unwillingness to cooperate with anyone else is astonishing.[43]

As Norbeck saw it, Borglum was himself a major obstacle to the Mount Rushmore project. As he grumbled to John Boland,

> Borglum will not consult with anyone. . . . I will have to take the matter entirely out of Borglum's hands. . . . If he had let us alone we would have had a meeting of the new commission before this time. . . . It is plain as day that Borglum is not satisfied to let anyone but himself handle it. . . . There will never be a Rushmore Memorial completed if Borglum is permitted to handle the business end of it. If he can be kept away from the business management and be kept good-natured 50% of the time, you will get along all right. . . . Borglum does not mean to make trouble.[44]

WORK STARTS AFRESH

As soon as members of the commission took their oaths of office, work resumed at full speed in the summer of 1929. Because the $250,000 was available retroactively, the first funds (which had already been spent in 1927), amounting to $54,670.56, could be matched. The commission, however, had a rigorous task facing them: How could they raise the nearly $200,000 to match the remainder of the federal authorization? Nevertheless, Rushmore buzzed with activity.

Progress on the mountain was gratifying to Borglum. His crew removed stone from the area between Washington's eyebrows to below the chin. As the drillers came within six inches of the intended surface of the face, dynamite blasting ended.

The second phase took place from scaffolds. Platforms with guard rails were bolted to stone or to steel projections on the granite surface. These scaffolds were considered safe and comfortable. In winter months canvas covers and wood-burning heaters on the platforms kept out the cold. At this stage, drilling was more shallow and spaced three or four inches apart. Chunks of rock between the holes were then wedged off with an air-driven flat tool called a channeling iron.

The final stage of work was done from wooden cages. The cages, manuevered by cables and winches, measured three-by-four feet for one man or three-by-eight feet for two men. The advantage of the cage was that it could fit into a sculpted eye or nostril. Pockmarked surfaces were "bumped" smooth with

YO-YO CRAZE TRIUMPHS OVER MOUNT RUSHMORE

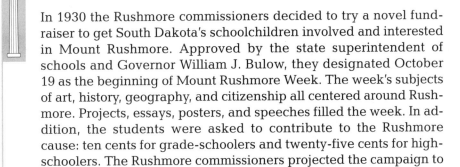

In 1930 the Rushmore commissioners decided to try a novel fundraiser to get South Dakota's schoolchildren involved and interested in Mount Rushmore. Approved by the state superintendent of schools and Governor William J. Bulow, they designated October 19 as the beginning of Mount Rushmore Week. The week's subjects of art, history, geography, and citizenship all centered around Rushmore. Projects, essays, posters, and speeches filled the week. In addition, the students were asked to contribute to the Rushmore cause: ten cents for grade-schoolers and twenty-five cents for high-schoolers. The Rushmore commissioners projected the campaign to yield ten thousand dollars.

However, the Mount Rushmore cause had competition in the form of a toy: the yo-yo. Debuting the week before, yo-yo mania swept the nation. A basic yo-yo cost ten cents while a fancy model cost twenty-five cents. During these depressed times, dimes and quarters were hard to come by. Choosing between Mount Rushmore, which was remote and speculative, and a yo-yo, which was a necessity of life, was not difficult for a child.

The unfortunate timing of the drive resulted in the collection of only seventeen hundred dollars since most of the students' dimes and quarters went to yo-yos.

Workers using stable cages and scaf-folds complete final stages of work, such as bumping the granite smooth.

another air-driven tool, called a dallet hand facer. Bumping gave the mountain carving a finished texture similar to concrete pavement.

The work cycle on each figure, then, consisted of measuring, drilling, blasting, more drilling, wedging, and bumping. On this massive project, the term *carving* was only a figure of speech.

In designing the figures, Borglum made allowances for erosion in centuries to come. For example, when sculpting Washington's nose, Borglum appraised the facial feature logically:

Granite in this location erodes at the rate of less than one inch in one hundred thousand years. After I heard that, I added a foot to Washington's nose. What is twelve inches on a nose to a face that is sixty feet in height? Twelve hundred thousand years, perhaps.[45]

Near the end of 1929, Washington's eyebrows, eyelids, eyeballs, and nose were almost ready to be bumped smooth. Granite was being blasted away for Jefferson's head, and space to the far right was being cleared for the entablature.

BOLAND TAKES CHARGE

The new commission had been sworn in, and its members were anxious to see the mountain portraits develop. John Boland, chair of the commission's executive committee, was in charge of finances. Boland had the important job of raising money and spending it wisely. Besides Borglum, Boland was the man whom the commission relied upon to keep progress going on Mount Rushmore.

Even though Boland considered his position an honor, many times he found himself in the undesirable position of deciding how money would be spent. He often incurred the wrath of Borglum with his financial decisions.

One of these decisions cost the project a valuable employee. Boland felt that Tucker's $10,000 annual salary was excessive and refused to pay him for 1928, which was a year when no work was done on the mountain. This decision infuriated Tucker. Furthermore, since Borglum did not come to his defense, Tucker also felt betrayed and consequently quit.

Tucker sued Borglum and the extinct Mount Harney Memorial Association—who wanted to pay him $833.33 ($10,000 divided by twelve months) for each of the months he actually worked in 1927. The association did not feel obligated to pay Tucker for the eighteen months when work was stopped, even though his contract entitled him to $10,000 per year. Boland wanted to keep the matter out of court and to have Tucker depart quietly and contentedly to avoid bad publicity. Thus, he arranged for a cash settlement of $7,500 to Tucker.

Borglum, who had counted on Tucker's daily presence and expertise, felt the loss keenly. As Borglum recalls, "When Mr. Tucker left, there was no saving the monument or the project except by my assuming all responsibility. I did that and I have done it to this moment; I expect to do it until the end of the work."[46]

HOW BIG ARE THESE SCULPTURES?

Borglum was invited to speak to a national audience on *Collier's Radio Hour*. During the address, he explained the pride he felt as he saw the giant portrait of Washington taking shape. This excerpt is from *Six Wars at a Time: The Life and Times of Gutzon Borglum, Sculptor of Mount Rushmore* by Howard Shaff and Audrey Karl Shaff.

A monument's dimensions should be determined by the importance to civilization of the events memorialized. . . . It is the greatness of the western world's adventure that gives us the subject matter for our colossal undertaking. . . . You ask how big these sculptures are? What does that matter? They are as big as the mountains and yet they are small compared to the great contribution to civilization they commemorate. . . . If they should sit in the [Niagara] falls this mighty river would only splash about their ears. If they should walk down the Hudson, they could barely creep under the great bridges . . . and when they reached the Statue of Liberty, they would have to stoop to read her dimming light.

Borglum appointed J. C. Denison, at $4,000 per year, to replace Tucker as superintendent. Even though Denison was reliable, skilled, and creative, he simply was not trained in mountain sculpture. Borglum decided to move his family to South Dakota so he could be on the site more often in order to give Denison close supervision.

Borglum bought a fifteen-hundred-acre cattle ranch near Hermosa, about twenty miles southeast of Rushmore. Unfortunately, this huge investment came just weeks before the October 24, 1929, stock market crash. This event shook the country and began a long era of depression, which affected Borglum's ability to get supplementary work and to pay off his debts. Although Borglum had completed many jobs and received large payments for them during 1928—he traveled fifty thousand miles that year—he still could not see his way out of debt. Borglum's wife, Mary, tried to help the situation by selling or mortgaging parts of a large estate they owned in Connecticut.

CREATIVE FINANCING

Many wealthy people lost everything when the stock market crashed; the private sources of money that Borglum and others had counted on therefore dried up completely. In January 1930, with only five thousand dollars in its treasury, the commission needed a plan. Borglum and his design/publicity committee sold advertising space in a thirty-six page folio-size brochure. The brochure contained pictures, a historical account of the project, an article by Borglum, President Coolidge's 1927 address, and other important documents and speeches.

The forty thousand copies generated national publicity and produced $10,000 in income that, when matched by the government, equalled $20,000. Another fund-raising plan was to form a booster club—the Mount Rushmore National Memorial Society. Memberships cost $100, and each member received a Borglum-autographed certificate. Fifty-six people joined the society, adding another $11,200 when combined with federal matching funds.

Meanwhile, Representative Williamson secured an additional appropriation of $60,000 from Congress, to be made available to match private contributions. Congressmen had to be assured that the state would build satisfactory roads and highways needed to reach the memorial. They were also skeptical that $250,000 would complete the project. Williamson assured them that more appropriations were not anticipated.

In the spring of 1930, with over $35,000 available, carving began again. Likewise, the Great Depression forced unemployment to skyrocket, leaving men eager to have any work. The new goal for Rushmore was to complete the Washington figure by July 4, the date Borglum had chosen for the dedication.

ENTABLATURE PLANS

Borglum hoped to expose part of the entablature at the dedication. He had modified his plans several times for its location. First, it was moved from the east wall to the west wall, where it was completely hidden by the faces. By 1930 Borglum had changed his mind again and relocated the entablature several hundred feet to the north of Washington's face. The "history" that would appear on the entablature was to be limited to five hundred words and would be composed of eight highlights.

By that spring, former president Calvin Coolidge had prepared the first couple of sections of the history and had sent them to Borglum. The first of these read: "THE DECLARATION OF INDEPENDENCE—The eternal right to seek happiness through self-government and the divine duty to defend that right at any sacrifice."[47] Borglum was displeased with the wording and altered it before releasing it to the press. The modified paragraph appeared in 317 newspapers in thirty-six states: "In the year of our Lord 1776 the people declared the eternal right to seek happiness, self-government and the divine duty to defend that right at any sacrifice."[48]

This unauthorized change offended and embarrassed Coolidge immensely. He renounced all responsibility for the content of the entablature and refused to write another word for it. He did not even attend the dedication of Washington's head.

RUSHMORE ATTRACTS TOURISTS

Due to the publicity from the entablature controversy, the monument became a popular tourist stop that summer. A road was built from Rapid City to Keystone and extending along the base of the mountain. On some days as many as four hundred cars jammed the two-lane highway.

Borglum himself was a major tourist attraction, and he did not disappoint visitors. He usually was on the mountain in a bosun's seat or in his studio working on his twenty-four-foot-high clay models. He was a memorable figure, often dressed in a business suit, neck scarf, and a Stetson hat.

UNVEILING WASHINGTON

In keeping with Borglum's taste, an elaborate dedication ceremony was planned to unveil the depiction of Washington. Mary
Borglum helped local women sew a seventy-two-by-forty-foot

*Using a photograph of the mountain, Borglum superimposed his concep-
tion of the entablature and inscription. This engraving, in the shape of the
territory gained through the Louisiana Purchase, never came about.*

On July 4, 1930, a large crowd attended the dedication of the sixty-foot Washington face, shown here veiled by the American flag.

American flag. The flag was then suspended lengthwise above Sixth Street in downtown Rapid City to publicize the dedication. One side of the flag was attached to the eighth story of the Alex Johnson Hotel and the other to a mast atop the Duhamel Building across the street. The huge banner barely cleared the ground with room below for passing traffic. Prior to July 4, the flag was moved to the mountain to shroud Washington's portrait.

Twenty-five hundred people came to the dedication. Senator Norbeck, however, was not among them. He had had surgery for mouth cancer the preceding September. To help take his mind off his illness, he was traveling with his family in Scandinavia that summer.

The dedication ceremony was staged to be impressive, and it was. The huge flag hid Washington's sixty-foot face from the spectators. From the stage at Doane Mountain, the viewers watched as, at a signal, the flag was slowly rolled up by cables attached to the mountaintop winches. To keep the flag from

THE CHANGING SEASONS

The weather often determined the progress of the work on the mountain. In *The Carving of Mount Rushmore*, Rex Alan Smith describes how the temperature affected workers in the different seasons.

Black Hills winters not being nearly as ferocious as the uninformed believed, there were many good days—and those that were good were the best of days. Facing to the southeast, the Rushmore cliff enjoyed maximum exposure to the sun and minimum exposure to the northwest winds, which were the coldest ones. . . . In the heat of summer, this sheltering [Rushmore's sixty-foot main crest] together with the reflection of sunlight from the white, fresh-cut rock created temperatures on the cliff's working face that were almost unbearable. But on the nice days of November and December when temperatures were in the 40s, 50s, and 60s, these same conditions provided a working climate that was almost ideal. In fact, on a day that was sun-bright and still, one could even work without suffering on the cliff in temperatures as low as, say, fifteen degrees above zero. . . .

Sun reflecting off the white granite rock made temperatures for the workers nearly unbearable in the summer, but ideal in fall and winter.

There were bad days too, of course, and just as the good days could be very, very good, the bad ones could be absolutely terrible. When the air was damp and raw and the sky was gray and the wind was a hostile living thing that probed the thickest clothing and made eyes water and turned feet into numbly aching lumps, working on the mountain became a matter of blind endurance. . . . [Workman] Red Anderson recalled, "Many times I'd come home so cold I wouldn't even eat supper. I'd just take a bunch of hot-water bottles and go to bed and try to get warm."

snagging, several workmen, suspended in bosun's seats, held the edges and "walked" it up. The audience was truly impressed at seeing both the stone portrait and the workmen, who appeared ant-size in the distance.

Borglum, introduced as the "foremost artist of the universe in colossal portraiture,"[49] proudly proclaimed,

> Let us place there, carved high, as close to heaven as we can, the words of our leaders, their faces, to show posterity what manner of men they were. Then breathe a prayer that these records will endure until the wind and the rain alone shall wear them away.[50]

Rifle salutes, roaring planes, and speeches left the crowd in awe.

The euphoria was fleeting, however. Three weeks after the unveiling, available funds were depleted and work closed down. J. C. Denison resigned, and William S. Tallman was appointed to replace him as superintendent. Tallman, a friend and former student of Borglum's who had worked as a pointer, would hold this new position for four years.

BACK TO THE MONEY GAME

In February 1931 the treasury of the Rushmore commission had a disappointing balance of $10.65. Borglum and Boland looked to the commissioners themselves for contributions. Irritated at being asked to contribute money instead of enjoying prestigious positions, a few resigned. But the dedicated ones stayed on, even more determined to see the project through to completion. Boland pressured the wealthy commission members to dip into their bank accounts, and $18,000 was collected. With matching funds and other incidental receipts, $43,280 was available for a spring start-up.

Borglum himself was not planning to be present for much of the next working season. During the summer of 1931, Borglum was scheduled to unveil his statue of Woodrow Wilson in Poznań, Poland. He hired Italian sculptor Hugo Villa, who had worked with him at Stone Mountain, to carry on the Rushmore work during his absence. Borglum's plan for this season was to finish Washington's face and carve down to his waist, complete with coat lapels. Jefferson's face was also to be roughed out. Borglum would return in late August, but to a controversy he had failed to anticipate.

CARVING CONTINUES

In spring and summer of 1931, while Borglum was away in Europe, Superintendent William Tallman and Hugo Villa made noticeable progress. Two men were assigned to Washington's portrait, and eight drillers worked on the Jefferson figure. Likewise, stone for the Lincoln head was in the preparation stages.

BORGLUM'S EMOTIONS FLARE

With Borglum gone, the crew was free to use as much dynamite as they wanted, which was always more than he allowed. When Borglum returned to Rushmore in late August, he was at first pleased with the results; however, a disagreement with Villa soon developed.

The dispute between Borglum and Villa was primarily about sculptural design. Villa and others felt strongly that placing Jefferson's face at Washington's right would not work, given the physical features of the stone. There was not enough granite to make it match the model. Others agreed with this assessment. A conflict about whether blasting had destroyed too much of the rock, or whether there had never been enough rock initially, remained unresolved.

The temperamental Borglum reacted fiercely to criticism of his portrait arrangement. Within two weeks after Borglum returned from Poland, he fired Villa. Borglum indignantly told John Boland, the treasurer and business manager of the Mount Rushmore Memorial Association, "I've never been criticized in my life by competent people, either here or abroad, never."[51]

Employees knew that it was difficult to work with Borglum, so they avoided him. It was professionally fatal to disagree with "the Old Man," as he was called behind his back. One anonymous employee, who worked many years on the mountain, remarked, "If the Old Man said it was going to rain and the sun was shining, I said, 'It sure looks like rain.'"[52] Borglum's habit of firing, then rehiring, employees was legendary. One fourteen-year employee, carver Merle Peterson, established a crew record of being fired and rehired eight times. Borglum's secretary at Rushmore, Jean Peters, topped even that record. She lost exact count after being fired and rehired ten times, but she estimated that it was about seventeen times.

Once employees adapted to Borglum's testy personality, they usually admired him. They may not have agreed with how he handled certain aspects of the project, such as his cautiousness with explosives, but the loyal crew was honored to be part of the memorial.

LINCOLN BECOMES PART OF THE CREW

After Villa was fired, Borglum pressed his son, Lincoln, to help out for a while. Lincoln describes how he became deeply involved in the Rushmore project, even though it cut short his plans to study engineering at the University of Virginia that fall:

With the Washington figure nearing completion and Jefferson's features progressing, the space for Lincoln is blasted for usable rock. Note the pointing machines atop Washington and Jefferson.

I reluctantly agreed. I'd had my heart set on college, but still the enormity of the work fascinated me, and I felt Dad really needed me. My first job was that of pointer, and I keenly felt its importance and responsibility.

We worked late into the fall—too late for me to go to school—so when the work started up again in the spring I was back on the job. Again fall came, the mountain made its demands, and again school was postponed. By that time I was completely caught up in the work and its message, so finally, in 1934, I gave up my plans for college altogether. Besides, after two years of no pay (my father could be a most persuasive man), I had made the payroll at last—55 cents an hour!

From then on I worked on the mountain until the work stopped for good in 1941, participating in every facet of the construction from the placing of explosive charges to operating the jackhammers. . . . I progressed to foreman, then superintendent of all construction work in 1938.[53]

THE REAL GUTZON BORGLUM

With the advantage of hindsight, author Rex Alan Smith gives the following description of Gutzon Borglum in his book *The Carving of Mount Rushmore.*

> He [Gutzon Borglum] was intense and serious, hard to joke with and impossible to joke at. Excepting wine with his meals he drank very little. He had no use for nightlife and never gambled. Self-centered though he was, he was a devoted family man who if he ever philandered left no trace of it. When in a rage his language was intemperate, but only mildly profane and never obscene. His work absorbed his energy, and aside from occasional fishing he seems never to have played very much nor even to have needed to. Exasperating as he often was to those around him, Borglum had an astonishing ability to hold their loyalty. Thus, even when his relations with them were stormy and strained, Norbeck, Williamson, Boland, Robinson, the crew at the mountain, and others continued to support him.

Assigning a prestigious pointer job to his son probably did not endear either Borglum or his son to the crew. However, Lincoln proved himself to the men. He had inherited a talent for art, and having observed his father, he had a sound understanding of sculpture. In addition, he was well liked by the men. As one crew member recalls,

> Lincoln always acted like a gentleman. Lincoln never let it go to his head. He didn't know much about what he was doing at first, but he was such a nice kid that all the other pointers helped him out until he learned to do it by himself, so it all worked out OK. Lincoln was a good guy to work with.[54]

Lincoln Borglum joins his father in the aerial tramway that traveled from the base of operations to the top of the Jefferson head.

During the 1930s, Lincoln Borglum also became Mount Rushmore's official photographer. The Eastman Kodak Company was experimenting with different film types and provided Lincoln with elaborate cameras and film. Carrying a camera at all times, the young man's candid photos appeared in newspapers, magazines, textbooks, and brochures. The photos helped create needed publicity in those lean years, when the Great Depression made money hard to obtain.

ON-AGAIN, OFF-AGAIN EMPLOYMENT

The scarcity of funds limited the work that could be done on Mount Rushmore. Throughout the depression, mountain work usually lasted less than six months a year. Even so, the Rushmore workers were better off than thousands of other South Dakotans who had no jobs and were on relief rolls. During the fourteen years of construction, the pay scale varied according to the skill level. On average, the hourly rate for unskilled workers was 50¢ to 60¢; for drillers, 75¢; for powdermen, $1; for carvers, $1.25; and for master pointer, $1.55.

Work stopped again in 1932 because there was no money to pay workers. Borglum used this shutdown to work on a statue of William Jennings Bryan, which was to be erected in Potomac Park in Washington, D.C. Then, in the fall, Senator Norbeck craftily obtained a fifty-thousand-dollar government grant to the state of South Dakota to hire unemployed workers. In this way, the federal government's New Deal attack on unemployment helped secure the future of Mount Rushmore National Memorial.

In 1933, under the Civilian Conservation Corps (CCC), fifty new workers landscaped the grounds at the foot of the mountain. (They did not work on the mountain itself, however, unless they came back another year after fulfilling their obligation as a CCC worker.) Under the federal matching funds program, Mount Rushmore received an additional fifty thousand dollars, which could be used for work on the mountain. With a total of one hundred thousand dollars, Mount Rushmore now had sound finances, but the lack of suitable rock in Jefferson's location would change the design plan.

CHANGES ON THE MOUNTAIN PLANS

The men had blasted about ninety feet off of the original surface. Blasting without the certainty of finding enough solid granite beneath the surface turned out to be a risky and expensive process. In terms of labor and materials, ten thousand dollars and eighteen months of hard work had been lost. The position of the Jefferson figure was eventually changed during the summer of 1934, but not before many tourists saw the original location.

After making dozens of sketches and models and shuffling and reshuffling the four figures, Borglum placed Jefferson to Washington's left. Setting Jefferson deep into the mountain freed the Washington figure and brought it out in full relief. This allowed the late afternoon sun to pass behind the Washington figure and light up the faces of Jefferson and Lincoln.

Another change in the plan was to relocate the entablature engraving to the back side of the mountain. The change in the entablature's placement was not publicized at first because the committee did not want to upset Coolidge's friends still in Congress and risk losing federal appropriations.

Some observers were discouraged by the changes in plans and thought such changes wasted money and time. Borglum reassured critics many times, saying it was "practically impossible to prepare and complete a fixed or final model which could be followed. . . . The design of this colossal work is subject to constant changes as the uncovering of stone progresses."[55]

Even minor deviations from the plan could be controversial. For example, when Borglum announced in October 1933 that he planned to turn Washington's head, citizens candidly voiced their displeasure. After scolding his critics, Borglum explained that he was not going to actually move the head, but merely carve the shoulders so that it would appear that the head was turned. The controversies, though, created publicity, which Borglum hoped would translate into steady funding.

FATHER-TO-SON NOTES

In Mount Rushmore: The Story Behind the Scenery, Lincoln Borglum explains that his father was always in command. Even when the sculptor planned to be absent, he confidently left notes for his son and the pointing crew to carry out.

I want you, in beginning the work and allotting the positions to the men, to avoid the two finished faces completely. Do not touch the hairlines around the face of Washington or his chin, or under his chin. Do not approach the face lines of Jefferson, or to the side of his face or under his chin.

On photograph No. 1, I have drawn a circle where you can locate Payne to begin down-drilling under what will be Washington's ear and the left-hand lapel of his coat. Put one or two men on the lapel, which I have marked No. 2. Put two men on Washington's shoulders and work carefully from the top, which I have marked No. 3. That will dispose of five or six men.

I have marked Lincoln's eye. You can put two men in cages in each of the eyes. I would use Anderson on the one side and Bianco on the other, putting Bianco where the feldspar streaks run down, and Anderson on the outside. I would give Payne, with Bianco, a position on the nose and have them begin to take off stone by drilling in squares and breaking it off down to within six or seven inches of the finished surface. But do not try to cut the eyelid or eyeball. Make a round mass for each of these. Lincoln's face in that way will take up probably six more men.

RUSHMORE ATTRACTS COAST-TO-COAST INTEREST

Meanwhile, improved roads substantially increased the number of tourists visiting the site. Crowds were estimated at 100,000 in 1931; 108,000 in 1932; and 135,000 in 1933. Senator Norbeck played a leading role in making sure that the new highways wound through the scenic beauty of the Harney National Forest en route to the monument, especially Iron Mountain Road. Three different tunnels frame a view of Mount Rushmore several miles away; other tunnels wind through granite pinnacles. Increased tourism meant that some organization needed to take charge of the memorial.

THE INNOCENCE OF TOURISTS

In Gilbert Fite's *Mount Rushmore*, writer Robert J. Dean relates an encounter when he and Borglum approached a man who was renting small telescopes to tourists at a lookout point on Iron Mountain some four miles from Rushmore.

"How's business?" Borglum inquired. "Good," the man said laconically. "What do the people say when they look at the mountain?" Borglum asked. The man looked at him quizzically. "You're Mr. Borglum, the sculptor, aren't you?" he asked, and when Borglum nodded, he went on cautiously, "Well, some say one thing and some say another." "Of course," Borglum agreed pleasantly. "But what do they say most often?" "I guess I'd better not say any more," the man answered, and his lips closed in a firm thin line.

"You'd really do me a great favor if you'd tell me," Borglum assured him. . . . "You're sure you won't get mad?" he said. "No, No!" Borglum said. "I can take the worst you've got."

"Well," the man said hesitantly. "I guess since you've asked it as a favor, I owe it to you to tell you. If it wasn't for you I wouldn't be in business. Most folks want to know how much concrete it took." . . .

Borglum asked, "And what do you tell them?" "I tell them I don't rightly know," the man said earnestly. "How much did it take?"

Therefore, in June 1933 President Franklin Roosevelt placed Mount Rushmore under the jurisdiction of the National Park Service in the Department of the Interior. The purpose of this action was to ensure funding availability. Since Arno B. Cammerer, director of the National Park Service, did not believe in elaborate works of man competing with nature, problems lay ahead. However, this move did not change the position or the responsibility of the commission.

The problem of what should appear on the entablature remained, though. The law stipulating that Coolidge was to compose the wording for the entablature was still in force, although Coolidge had recently died. In February 1934 the Hearst newspaper chain publicized a contest for a six-hundred-word history of the United States. The contest suggested that the winning essay would be carved on Mount Rushmore.

A total of 847,705 texts were submitted from coast to coast. Cash and medals were awarded in many categories, ranging from grammar school to college. The grand winner was John Edward Bradley, although his essay was never carved on Mount Rushmore. However, the college division winner, William Andrew Burkett from the University of Nebraska, Omaha, law school, later paid to have his entry engraved on a bronze plaque. In 1975 the six-foot-by-seven-and-a-half-foot plaque was installed by the National Park Service at the Borglum Viewing Terrace.

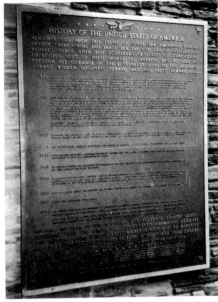

The primary purpose of the contest was to generate publicity for the monument. South Dakota's Senator William J. Bulow pointed out that "a million dollars could not have purchased the advertising thus produced."[56]

William Andrew Burkett, the college division winner of the 1934 essay contest, had his entry engraved on this plaque.

During the summer of 1934, Senator Norbeck was instrumental in obtaining amended federal legislation that dropped the "matching funds" clause and provided for funding by direct government appropriation. Once the government assumed the entire financial burden, work only halted in bad weather. But government regulations would be a thorn in Borglum's side and affect relationships between the sculptor and people who followed rules.

BORGLUM VERSUS BOLAND

One such relationship was with Boland, who handled finances. The association between the two men gradually disintegrated, especially after 1935. Their personalities—one erratic and wasteful, the other thrifty and methodical—resulted in great conflict. Boland insisted that government regulations be followed, and Borglum disregarded restrictions if they hindered his work.

Borglum and Boland differed on the purchase and use of equipment. Borglum wanted a power plant, a new compressor, more drills, and an aerial tramway for workers. Boland refused and explained his practical point of view: "The additional cost of machinery for the increase in power would materially cut down the total man hours of drilling and carving . . . and thereby result in less productive work and efficient expenditures."[57]

The tension between Boland and Borglum affected others as well. Because Superintendent Tallman sided with Boland on most issues, Borglum accused him of disloyalty, leading to Tallman's resignation in 1935.

Borglum had come to see the monument as part of his very existence, and he was protective of the Rushmore project. He also feared that another incomplete venture like Stone Mountain would reflect unfavorably on his professional status.

THE JEFFERSON FIGURE

Work progressed despite all the conflict. In the spring of 1934, thirty men were hired, most of whom worked on Jefferson. A primary problem with the Jefferson head was refitting it on the mountain to avoid a five-foot-wide fissure on the nose. Borglum feared that this crack could cause the nose to break off in five hundred or five thousand years. Borglum explains his concern:

> Jefferson's nose at the right-hand nostril has one of these cracks. When I started or rather located Jefferson's head the crack ran across the end of it. I reset the head five degrees to the north, set it back four feet, then tilted the head about eighteen inches. Finally the crack just escaped the right-hand nostril; it still cuts down across the

Men in cages and on scaffolds detail features of Jefferson's face. The back of Washington's head has not yet been separated from the mountain.

right eye, past the nose and upper lip and through the middle of the chin. In that location, it is perfectly harmless because it is supported by all the mountain back of it, and can be easily seamed against moisture.[58]

Jefferson's cracked lip was patched by Luigi Del Bianco, an expert stonecutter. He used a solid piece of granite twenty-four inches tall, ten inches wide, and ten inches deep. The patch is held in place by pins and is difficult to detect. It is the only patch on the entire sculpture.

Most observers wanted Borglum to fully complete each head before starting on another, but different types of positioning problems proved that it was better to locate the faces before finishing any one of them. Borglum endured much criticism because outsiders did not understand this process of making certain that the individual figures would fit together in an integrated whole.

APPROPRIATION SQUEAKS BY

In 1935 Congress granted a two-hundred-thousand-dollar appropriation for Mount Rushmore. Passage of the bill was difficult since the Great Depression was still limiting available money. Some representatives argued that an incomplete monument with only Washington and Jefferson was acceptable. Others suggested that government funds should be spent on the necessities of life and for helping South Dakota farmers who were in greater need of money than of a monument. A few members of Congress, however, felt that this amount was a pittance in comparison to the ten billion dollars that Congress had appropriated "for God knows what,"[59] as they characterized Roosevelt's New Deal programs.

NEW PERSONNEL

In 1936 another personality was added to the project's team. Julian C. Spotts, a resident engineer for the National Park Service was assigned to Mount Rushmore. At first, this addition appeared to please everyone. With the appointment of Spotts, Borglum thought he could dodge Boland and the commission; likewise, Boland looked at the appointment as a buffer between himself and Borglum. Spotts made many changes that pleased Borglum, such as upgrading the tram so that it could haul workers, increasing air-compressor capability, and improving buildings.

Despite these improvements, Borglum balked at Spotts's insistence on conforming to National Park Service regulations. For example, Borglum refused to supply the Department of the Interior with specific data such as an outline of operations, a personnel roster, or pipeline efficiency and progress reports. Borglum roared his complaints: "It is difficult to find this unique work becoming the victim of petty bureaucratic entanglements."[60] Borglum even called Spotts a "brainless jelly bean."[61] By the end of summer, the two men were completely estranged and communicated only by letter, even though their offices were only a hundred feet apart.

Regardless of their administrative problems, a big celebration was planned for the unveiling of Jefferson on August 30, 1936, and President Roosevelt was scheduled to attend.

THE JEFFERSON DEDICATION

At the dedication of the Jefferson sculpture, Borglum set off blasts of dynamite to demonstrate how rock was removed. After the sixty-foot face was unveiled and a flag was hoisted, Borglum invited Roosevelt to speak. The president had not intended to make a speech, but Borglum pressed him to speak, so Roosevelt informally addressed the audience of about three thousand visitors. He said, "I had had no conception until about ten minutes ago not only of its [Mount Rushmore's] magnitude, but of its permanent beauty and of its permanent importance."[62]

President Roosevelt delivered his speech while seated in his open-top limousine. He talked about how inspiring the monument was and how it represented the privileges and blessings of freedom:

> I think we can meditate a little on those Americans ten thousand years from now when the weathering on the face of Washington and Jefferson and Lincoln shall have

EXPERT BLASTERS

In his article "Mountain Sculpture," which appeared in the January 1933 *Scientific American*, Gutzon Borglum describes the expertise and accuracy of the men who used dynamite to remove unusable granite on Rushmore.

> I ought to say here that we use high explosives in all proportions and in all quantities. I have two or three men—always more than one—who are not only experts in their knowledge of what an inch or six inches of dynamite will do, but who know what can be done with a percussion cap alone, even without the dynamite. Such a man must also know and be in constant touch with the drilling that is going on and with the general design; he knows the power of his explosive and the danger that may come to stone in place or to nearby work by using an overcharge. This empirical knowledge has proved of great value at Mount Rushmore, S.D.
>
> We have developed the drilling and blasting away of stone on Mount Rushmore to such a nicety that I can shape out a nose to within an inch or two of the finished surface, even down over the point of the nostrils, can shape out the lips, and grade the contours of the cheek and the brow and all curved surfaces. We can shape out even the eyeball as a whole, but the defining of the eyelids and pupils is done with a drill and the air tool, operated by hand.

At the August 30, 1936, dedication of the Jefferson sculpture, Borglum converses with Franklin D. Roosevelt after the president's impromptu speech.

proceeded to perhaps a depth of a tenth of an inch—
meditate and wonder what our descendants, and I think
they will still be here, will think about us. Let us hope
that at least they will give us the benefit of the doubt—
that they will believe we have honestly striven every day
and generation to preserve for our descendants a decent
land to live in and a decent form of government to operate under.[63]

Also in attendance at the unveiling was Senator Norbeck, who was now in the last stages of his illness from cancer of the tongue and jaw. When he died on December 20, Mount Rushmore lost one of its most devoted and protective backers. But thanks to Norbeck, Rushmore now was a federal project and sure to be completed.

TONS OF ROCK ARE BLASTED AWAY

During 1936 the brow, nose, and eyes of the Lincoln figure were detailed. In addition, tons of rock were blown off the mountain in preparation for carving the Roosevelt head. In fact, the drillers had to blast about eighty feet from the surface to find suitable granite. The large quantity of unusable rock caused Borglum to

Abraham Lincoln's granite face and features are detailed by the bumping process. His hair and beard are left textured.

fear he might have to omit the Roosevelt figure altogether because there was only thirty feet of rock left in front of a canyon.

Despite the progress made, controversy continued to plague the project. When the 1937 carving season began, the National Park Service expected a detailed list of accomplishments. Borglum swiftly reacted: "[The sculpture was] no boy's job, nor road contractor's job and is not, must not and cannot be the victim of engineer's rule and compass."[64]

Borglum was absent from Rushmore for most of the 1937 season, which helped minimize the conflict. However, he did spend a portion of the year camped in Washington, D.C., in an attempt to obtain a new contract for his services at Mount Rushmore. He was unsuccessful in convincing congressmen to increase his commission on expenditures from 25 percent to 30 percent, though. The main objection to Borglum's request was the lack of an overall plan of expenditures for completion of the mountain.

Despite the conflicts and setbacks, work on the mountain continued. Borglum's son, now foreman, worked well with Spotts. The season was spent completing work on Lincoln's face and roughing out Roosevelt.

THE DEDICATION OF ABRAHAM LINCOLN

Only a year after the Jefferson dedication, the Lincoln figure was ready for recognition. This rapid progress demonstrated the effect of ample funds and systematic management of the work.

Abraham Lincoln's dedication date of September 17, 1937, was chosen to coincide with the 150th anniversary of the adoption of the U.S. Constitution. Again, Borglum staged a dramatic event for the five thousand visitors.

As the last speaker at Doane Mountain, Borglum read a roll call of Mount Rushmore supporters who had died. The list included the familiar names of Calvin Coolidge, Charles E. Rushmore, and Senator Peter Norbeck. Following the reading, a bugler standing atop Washington's head played taps. Borglum's daughter, Mary Ellis, then signaled to her brother, who set off sticks of dynamite. When the explosions stopped, the huge American flag covering Lincoln's face was pulled aside. The program concluded with a vocal solo and a band playing "The Star-Spangled Banner."

The dedication of the Lincoln figure took place on September 17, 1937. Before an audience of five thousand people, Borglum read a roster of deceased supporters of the project that included Coolidge, Rushmore, and Norbeck.

SOUR RELATIONSHIPS

In 1938 Borglum decided to rid himself of both the National Park Service and the commission, including Boland. He refused to go to the mountain that spring and instead went to Washington, D.C., and lobbied everyone he knew to help him in his fight. Borglum had written to President Roosevelt and other officials in Washington complaining about everyone and everything: insufficient power, lack of a hoist for his men, failure of the commission to hire skilled carvers, and interference from Spotts and Boland.

All of his letters and complaints finally met with a positive response from Congress. He won a sweeping victory, which included back payment for his expenses, a new commission, a large monetary authorization for the project, and freedom from bureaucracy.

Borglum recommended names to Roosevelt for a new commission, which would rubber-stamp his requests. The old commission was asked to resign and the National Park Service was relieved of all responsibility for the monument. Congress authorized an appropriation of three hundred thousand dollars to continue work on the mountain.

Spotts and others in the National Park Service were happy to be unburdened of the project, which they felt was contrary to the agency's mission. As for John Boland, although he had found working with Borglum troublesome, he resented the decision since he had been a strong Rushmore backer for nine years. However, the memorial needed Borglum more than it needed Boland. Borglum's triumph over his opponents tempted him to begin work on a lavish, yet unapproved, addition to the monument. This new idea, too, would hit snags.

GRAND PLANS SHATTER

In June 1938 Borglum received fifty thousand dollars of the three-hundred-thousand-dollar appropriation from the government. With Boland and the National Park Service out of the way, he was untroubled by outside interference. With his authority unchallenged, he went directly to work on a project that he had been dreaming about: a Hall of Records to preserve the cultural achievements of America.

ARCHIVES IN A CAVE

This elaborate and ambitious repository was to be located in a canyon behind the figures. Borglum planned the cave-like hall to be one hundred feet deep, eighty feet wide, and thirty-two feet high. The interior of the hall would contain twenty-five statues of important American men and women. Permanent scrolls would list American achievements and inventions in such fields as art, literature, medicine, and science.

In Borglum's vision, future generations would climb an eight-hundred-foot-high granite stairway. The fifteen-foot-wide grand stairway would start at Doane Mountain and wind around behind Lincoln's head to the entrance of the hall. This timeless monument and hall would allow visitors to learn about the granite faces and other American accomplishments.

Borglum's vast plans shocked most people, including his handpicked commission. They worried that the sculpted faces would not be completed if Borglum put all his energies and money into the Hall of Records. By this time Borglum was nearly seventy-two years old, and many people were concerned about his deteriorating health.

Aware of his own limitations, Borglum appointed his son, Lincoln, as superintendent in 1938. Lincoln handled administrative duties and supervised the daily work on Roosevelt as well.

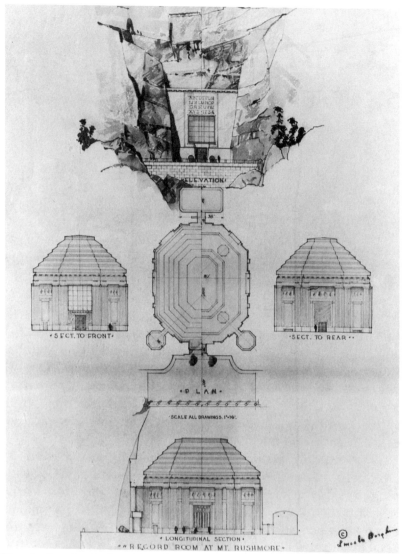

Lincoln Borglum's drawings showed his father's vision of the Hall of Records, which included mosaic walls, a bronze and glass door, busts of great Americans, and aluminum scrolls of historical records.

In July 1938 the enthusiastic Borglum began excavation for the Hall of Records, spending sixteen thousand dollars on the project. He blasted a tunnel sixty-eight feet deep, twenty feet high, and twelve feet wide before stopping work to concentrate most of his carvers on the Roosevelt face in preparation for a July 2, 1939, dedication.

The 1938–1939 season was productive and long. Borglum's crews worked the entire winter, except for three weeks during which the temperature dipped to twenty degrees below zero. To help keep the men warm, Borglum covered the scaffolds with waterproof canvas and heated the enclosure by using steel drums filled with burning wood.

MEET GLENN BRADFORD, MOUNT RUSHMORE CARPENTER

Glenn Bradford, now age eighty-five, worked on Mount Rushmore during the summer of 1939. Bradford was twenty-six at the time, and he worked primarily on President Theodore Roosevelt's mustache and chin area. As an apprentice carpenter, he built many ladders and scaffolds and had the opportunity to meet Borglum, along with many other workers on the mountain.

During an October 5, 1998, interview in Rapid City, South Dakota, Bradford reminisced about his experiences at Rushmore.

> Borglum was an eccentric man and he wanted you to know that he was boss and you had to do things his way. Even though another person made suggestions, Borglum would twist it around so it was his idea. He was all right to work for. Everybody tried to keep out of his way so they wouldn't get fired. . . . Lincoln was a prince of a guy. You could talk to him and he'd talk back to you. Not so with Gutzon.

Carpenter Glenn Bradford built scaffolds.

> The workers on the mountain were all ages. One man was seventy. Borglum felt sorry for the old man because he had a string of children to support. About 150 to 200 men worked the summer that I worked. Fifteen jackhammer operators worked at one time. Most of the workers were former miners. They knew how to run a jackhammer, but they had to be trained on depth drilling techniques. They didn't like to wear respirator masks because within a half hour the masks were clogged with dust.

As work progressed, Borglum moved to convince Congress to protect the monument and its surroundings. The Mount Rushmore Act of 1938 set aside fifteen hundred acres of the Harney National Forest and designated the land as the Mount Rushmore Memorial Reservation. In 1940 Borglum convinced Congressman Francis Case to sponsor a bill adding three hundred acres to the reservation.

ONE STEP FORWARD, ONE STEP BACK

By February 1939 the $50,000 appropriation had been spent, and again Borglum approached the federal government for the $250,000 appropriation left in the Mount Rushmore account. Although the money had been appropriated, it still needed to be approved by a congressional subcommittee before it could be released. The congressional representatives now began to question how long this project would drag on, and they wanted a completion deadline. They gave Borglum the entire $250,000 on the condition that the sculpture be finished by June 1940.

Borglum rejoiced in his new circumstances. With the largest budget in Rushmore's history, Borglum planned to hire a large crew in the spring of 1939. In May Borglum's joy was shattered. President Roosevelt sent him news of a general government reorganization plan. Under this plan control of Rushmore would be returned to the National Park Service as of July 1. Naturally, Borglum was furious; the National Park Service was also unhappy with the arrangement. Although Borglum met with Roosevelt, he failed to change the president's mind. Borglum criticized the president's action, claiming the order "put me right back where I was, at the mercy of unsympathetic men who have no idea of how life can be given to blocks of granite."[65]

THE NATIONAL PARK SERVICE SETS GOALS

Borglum complained that National Park Service employees were uninterested and ignorant of his needs. The Department of the Interior, which supervised the National Park Service, did not relish this assignment either. Harold L. Ickes, secretary of the interior, indicated how he felt at the time:

> When I have anything official to do in connection with Gutzon Borglum's enterprise at Mount Rushmore I always feel like equipping myself as a man does when he

Harold L. Ickes, secretary of the interior, compared the unpleasant task of working with Borglum to the chore of moving a hive full of bees.

fusses with a beehive. Mr. Borglum has customarily made it so unpleasant . . . that I groaned all night following the day when I learned that the Mount Rushmore National Memorial Commission had been sent here for administration.[66]

An early decision by the Department of the Interior focused all efforts on ensuring that the faces were completed while Borglum was still alive. Work on the Hall of Records could be delayed and even done by National Park Service employees and artists, if necessary, but the carving of the figures could only be completed by Borglum. The National Park Service allowed Borglum to keep Lincoln in place as superintendent, however.

Borglum was equally disappointed when his own hand-picked commission insisted that he complete the four presidential figures before working on the Hall of Records. This suggestion was given added urgency when it was discovered that the men working in the cavern were in grave danger of contracting silicosis, a disease caused by inhaling the fine dust created by drilling deep inside the cave. Thus, work on the hall was temporarily suspended—a suspension which eventually turned out to be permanent. Many years later, two former workers died of the slow-evolving disease.

SCULPTURAL COUPS

As the figure of Theodore Roosevelt neared completion, Borglum scored a sculptural coup through his treatment of the president's famous spectacles. Rather than sculpting highly visible spectacles, Borglum planned to provide just a suggestion of a frame. The carving required only a nosepiece and two ridges across each of Roosevelt's upper cheeks. The sculptor's treatment of Roosevelt's glasses was one innovation; his treatment of the figures' eyes was another.

Using a rare finishing feature, the four faces portray lifelike eyes. Borglum studied the faces from many viewpoints—the tramway cage, Doane Mountain, in the canyon, and through his

(Left) Borglum simulated Roosevelt's spectacles by carving only a nosepiece and two ridges across the upper cheeks. (Right) The protruding shaft from Jefferson's right eye gives expression to the eye when viewed at a distance.

 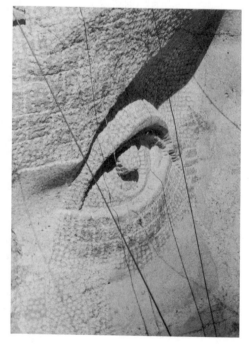

studio windows. He observed the faces in the angled light of dawn, midday, and in evening shadows. As a result, each iris is carved deep and is several feet across. Forming each pupil is a granite shaft measuring about eight by eight by twenty-two inches. From a distance, these jutting granite shafts are seen as points of light and add expression and character to the eyes.

THE ROOSEVELT DEDICATION

The dedication of the Roosevelt figure coincided with the fiftieth anniversary of South Dakota's statehood. Twelve thousand people attended the dedication, which was held on a starlit evening. Eighty-three-year-old Doane Robinson was there, wearing the same swallow-tailed coat and derby hat that he had worn fifty years earlier at the ceremony in which South Dakota had become a state. A *Newsweek* article describes the Roosevelt dedication, along with the monument's longevity:

> As fireworks sizzled across the night sky, moonlight and floodlights combined to illuminate all the great stone faces for the first time. . . . Since under normal atmospheric conditions granite erodes only an inch every 100,000 years, the four portraits have a life expectancy of from 2,000,000 to 3,000,000 years.[67]

The magazine overestimated the monument's life; it is now known that granite weathers one inch every ten thousand years.

Additional frustrations for Borglum followed the dedication. He refused to let go of his grandiose ideas, although it had become clear that the appropriated three hundred thousand dollars would not cover expenses needed to finish the figures, let alone the grand stairway, Hall of Records, and the entablature. Borglum had already given up on the west wall inscription and decided to place it instead in the Hall of Records. He explained why he insisted on a written record of the significance of Mount Rushmore: "You might as well drop a letter into the world's postal service without an address or signature, as to send that carved mountain into history without identification."[68]

Borglum's December 1939 annual report to the National Park Service made clear his frustration: "It is little short of absurd to apply roadbuilder practices or sophomoric engineering to the

Fireworks explode in the evening sky during the July 2, 1939, dedication of the final figure, Theodore Roosevelt.

carving of a great portrait; it is precisely this kind of interference that is and has been the only persistent enemy of this memorial." [69]

LET YOUR FINGERS FEEL

Despite Borglum's complaints, work proceeded. At this stage, the figures still needed more shaping: Jefferson and Roosevelt below the chin, and Lincoln below the beard. In addition, fine finishing of all four faces was scheduled. This process was Borglum's strongest point. He trained his carvers to use five-foot-long molded masks of each face for working on details. These masks were stored inside the winch houses and were suspended from the mountaintop for reference as the men worked. According to Borglum, "If you *feel* the mask . . . close your eyes or put it behind you, just *feel* it—your fingers will tell you much more about what you are supposed to be doing than your eyes will."[70]

The mounds, hollows, and wrinkles that were transferred from the masks not only gave the stone faces character and personality but also showed the genius of Borglum and the craftsmanship of his men. For this feat, Borglum would long be honored by the world as a great sculptor.

DISAPPOINTMENTS

The year 1940 was one of discouragement, anger, unhappiness, and ill health for Borglum. Strenuous living had taken its toll on

WORKERS' SAFETY RECORD

Only two accidents occurred during the carving of the Mount Rushmore project. One happened during a 1936 summer thunderstorm in nearby Keystone. A bolt of lightning struck the dynamite that was being prepared by a driller on the mountain. The man was flung out into the air on his cable, but he flexed his knees to keep from breaking his legs when he crashed back against the mountain. Likewise, a nearby driller's shoe was blown off, but he was happy to still have his feet! After that incident, mountain work ceased during thunderstorms.

The second, and most serious, accident took place on June 2, 1940. Five workmen were riding in the tramway cage to the top of the mountain when a shear pin in the cable pulley broke. As the tram shot fifteen hundred feet down the mountain, the men jumped on the emergency brake, causing it to crack and break off. Luckily, a composed foreman who was in the hoist house quickly stuck a two-by-four board against the spinning cable drum, which slowed the descent. All of the tram's riders, except for one man, had minor injuries. This unfortunate man, Norman "Happy" Anderson, had jumped from the tram. His mishap was recalled in T. D. Griffith's *America's Shrine of Democracy*.

I remember the last thing on my mind was that I would jump and hit the roof of the compressor house." . . . Anderson recalled. "I broke my left arm, all the ribs on my left side, my collar bone, and my insides were busted open so I couldn't eat. Of course, I didn't know anything about that for nine days 'til I came to.

Borglum, but his son, Lincoln, now artistically and administratively skilled, continued to work diligently on refining the faces.

Again more money was required to complete the memorial. On May 15, 1940, the Department of the Interior submitted a request to the Bureau of the Budget for $350,000. This estimate included moneys for the faces, stairway, Hall of Records, landscaping, and miscellaneous improvements. However, the bureau only approved $86,000 for 1941.

Congress had grown tired of Borglum's unkept promises and vowed that this was their final allotment to the memorial. Also, lawmakers were now concerned with world affairs. Europe was at war, and there were indications that the United States would soon be involved. Federal money now had to be preserved for defense of the nation.

In February 1941 Borglum went to Chicago for prostate surgery. Although the surgery went well, Borglum fought his last battle on March 6. He developed a blood clot and died in the hospital.

LINCOLN TAKES OVER

After Borglum's death, the commission recommended his son, Lincoln, as permanent superintendent. At that time, all remaining functions of the commission were transferred to the National Park Service. No money had been appropriated for work after July 1, 1941, but twenty-one thousand dollars remained in the treasury. Lincoln Borglum had the workers concentrate on the facial features of Roosevelt, refining Lincoln's head, blocking out Jefferson's collar, and completing the collar and lapels of Washington's coat. Operations continued until funds were exhausted on October 31.

The mountain lapsed into silence at four o'clock that day. In November the machinery was stored, most of the buildings on the mountaintop were dismantled, the cableway was removed, and general cleanup tasks were undertaken. As Lincoln states in his final report,

> I do not think any more should be done on figures of the Memorial. It looks very well as it is and I think it is more effective this way, than if carried down as shown on the models. . . . I believe that it is very essential that the Hall of Records and the stairway leading to it, be completed."[71]

GRANITE DUST

When men left the mountain at the day's end, they carried one problem with them: granite dust. Although most of it had been blown off by blasts of high-pressure air from a nozzled hose before they trooped down the steps, some still remained. In *The Carving of Mount Rushmore*, Rex Alan Smith describes the problems that granite dust presented.

Drillers did not like wearing face masks because they became clogged with dust within fifteen to thirty minutes.

> The remainder [dust], clinging to hair and skin, the men wear home with them. The dust makes hair dry and strawlike and almost impossible to pull a comb through, and it makes clothing rasp against the skin. A man can wash it off, once he gets home, but even that is not easy. It catches at the soap and resists being lubricated by it, and only with much soap and effort can it be dislodged. And that is but the dust's exterior effect. The interior effect of that which a man has breathed is something he cannot yet know, but in years to come he likely will find it out. Many of the men, Lincoln Borglum among them, will wind up with permanently scarred lungs. Some will ultimately develop silicosis; in 1948 James Champion, Jr., will die of it, and in 1955 Elton "Hoot" Leach will do the same. At the moment, however, that lies in the unknown future. Presently the dust is only an irritating nuisance to be dealt with before enjoyment of the evening can begin.

The National Park Service, however, showed no interest in these projects.

UNFINISHED PROJECTS

Borglum's dream for Mount Rushmore had included the entablature and the Hall of Records. The entablature, or inscription, was to describe eight crucial events in U.S. history from 1776 to

1904—Washington to Roosevelt. This plan was abandoned for a number of reasons. First, in order for the letters to be legible from any distance, they would have had to be so large that there would not be room for five hundred words. Second, the area where the entablature was to appear was needed for the Lincoln head because Jefferson's location had changed.

Work on the Hall of Records was suspended in 1939 because it was feared that men working on it would develop silicosis. The shallow entryway that was blasted into the rock is now home to a historical records chamber set in the floor and sealed by a granite capstone.

The presidents' figures were never completed to the waist as the models showed. Due to the shortage of labor and materials caused by World War II, the National Park Service declared the monument completed. The massive pile of blasted rubble remains at the foot of the mountain. Even though Gutzon Borglum did not live to see the refined memorial, he at least knew his ambition to carve a massive tribute to freedom had been realized.

EPILOGUE

Although Gutzon Borglum may not have been America's finest sculptor, he was the most unusual and the boldest artist of his time. Mount Rushmore is considered one of the world's great monuments. In size alone, it is unsurpassed; the entire head of the Great Sphinx at Giza—from its chin to the top of its head—is not quite as long as Washington's nose! The mountain is also considered an unparalleled engineering feat.

In a January 1947 article in the *Saturday Evening Post,* William J. Bulow, who served as governor of South Dakota and in the U.S. Senate, reflects on Gutzon Borglum's ability:

William J. Bulow became linked with the Rushmore project in 1927 as chairman of the Mount Harney Memorial Association.

> No other man has ever had the perspective to carve such gigantic figures and make them look natural to the human eye from any spot below. Several times I climbed into the basket and rode up the cable to the mountaintop and inspected the carvings. . . . The close-up view is disappointing. You cannot see the face of Lincoln when you stand on his lower eyelid; you cannot see Washington while walking back and forth on his lower lip. It takes a genius to figure out the proper perspective so that the carvings will look right from the point from which the human eye beholds them. Gutzon Borglum was that genius.[72]

THE COST

The total cost of creating the Mount Rushmore National Memorial was $989,992.32. The federal government paid $836,000 of this total, but the rest came from private donations. Borglum received a total salary of about $170,000 over the sixteen years that he was involved with the memorial. This amount came to less than $11,000 a year. As Lincoln Borglum notes,

> Fame is compensation of a kind, and the mountain did assure my father his place in history. . . . For Rushmore captured the imagination not of an individual, a city, state, or region, but of an entire nation. And that was the result he had worked for; today he would feel repaid many times over if he could see the throngs who come to

view the memorial each day. He never valued money highly anyway; he thought it should not even be a prime consideration when a great *idea* was under discussion.[73]

THE PROFITS

Mount Rushmore has turned out to be a sound investment for the federal government. In the late 1990s about 2.6 million people visited the monument yearly. Although admission to the memorial is free, federal taxes on gasoline sold to motorists visiting the memorial amounts to millions of dollars each year.

The state of South Dakota has also profited immensely from tourism, just as Doane Robinson and Senator Peter Norbeck envisioned. Although South Dakota's legislature never appropriated money for the monument, it did spend money building highways to the memorial and on advertising. Because of this modest investment, hundreds of people hold jobs directly related to the presence of the memorial. Likewise, over the years the monument has brought hundreds of millions of tourists' dollars into the state's treasury.

By 1950, families such as this one were bringing tourist dollars into South Dakota.

MOUNT RUSHMORE WORKERS

A total of almost four hundred workers were employed at Mount Rushmore over the fourteen-year period. This number includes secretaries and the women who worked in the cookhouse and bunkhouse. Nineteen surviving Rushmore workers were honored guests at a fiftieth anniversary event held on July 3, 1991, which was attended by President George Bush and other representatives of local, state, and federal governments.

After his father's death, Lincoln Borglum became the first National Park Service superintendent at Mount Rushmore and remained in that position until 1944. He then moved to La Feria, Texas, where he continued to work as a sculptor until he died in 1986.

MOUNT RUSHMORE TODAY

The Mount Rushmore Memorial Reservation has been reduced to 1,278 acres; 500 acres became part of the Norbeck Wildlife Preserve. Although the monument was initially only visible in daylight, the first floodlights were installed in 1950, allowing evening visitors a heavenly view of the presidents. In 1992 a six-year, $56-million improvement project began. Donations, private investments, and fuel taxes paid for enhanced visitor accommodations and administrative facilities, which were dedicated on June 15, 1998.

To help visitors grasp the full meaning of what is often called "the Shrine of Democracy," the National Park Service provides exhibits of tools used in construction and other artifacts, photographs, orientation talks, and a brief movie about the mountain carving.

MONUMENT MAINTENANCE

Although the hard granite of the Rushmore memorial is extremely resistant to weather, cracks caused by natural forces could eventually damage the carving. The monument is inspected each fall by National Park Service employees who are strapped into harnesses and lowered by a hand-operated winch to check and repair any cracks that have developed. One winch is located on the top of each figure's head for this maintenance purpose. Borglum himself devised a compound of linseed oil, white lead, and powdered granite for sealing cracks. In 1990 this concoction was replaced by an elastic watertight silicone compound made by Dow Corning. Once the sealant has been placed, it is sprinkled with granite dust so it blends in with the rest of the surface.

Visitors might see wide bands of discolored rock on the faces, but these are natural to the granite and are not patches. Rain and melting snow wash any dirt off the figures, and the bleaching action of the sun gives the faces a white appearance. No other cleaning is necessary.

In preparation for the fiftieth anniversary of the monument's completion, the Mount Rushmore National Memorial Society hired a geotechnical consulting firm, RE/SPEC, to conduct the first detailed survey of the structure.

Three hundred close-range photographs were used to make a three-dimensional computer image of the mountain faces. As a result, 140 cracks were identified, measured, and mapped, with 21 of them listed as critical. Some of these cracks may need to be stabilized with pins.

RECORDS IN A BURIED CRYPT

As reported in the Rapid City *Journal* on August 10, 1998, the previous day 119 people watched as Borglum's descendants, along with federal, state, and local officials, installed a crypt in the entryway to the Hall of Records. Sixteen porcelain enamel panels bearing the written history of Rushmore and the 150 years spanned by Rushmore's presidents were placed in the crypt by National Park Service workers. During the ceremony Mary Ellis Borglum Vhay said that the records chamber was "the fulfillment of my father's dream."

The newspaper article gives more details of the event.

A view from inside the uncompleted Hall of Records.

Rushmore Superintendent Dan Wenk said that the memorial's master plan always allowed for completing the records hall, provided that federal funds were not used and construction passed environmental and historical standards. The studies concluded in 1994. But the huge underground complex Gutzon Borglum proposed would have cost "millions and millions," and completing it would have overshadowed the past.

In an October 1998 photograph, a melting snowfall enhances the discolored bands of rock on the presidents' faces. In the foreground, state flags decorate the walkway to the visitor center.

PUBLIC REACTIONS

The monument was open to the public during all stages of the work, and from the beginning the project was controversial. Some observers felt that the carving was a "type of mutilation of the noble outlines of the mountains."[74] New York art critic Ralph M. Pearson did not share Borglum's ideas about art and dismissed the aesthetic value of his work. He referred to the monument as "monstrous naturalistic heads" and considered carving into the mountain "vandalism, discord, a kind of blasphemy."[75]

However, a day spent at Mount Rushmore listening to ordinary citizens' comments suggests that few people share these sentiments. People see more than just stone faces at Rushmore—they are reminded of the qualities that they believe characterize America: freedom, justice, equality, and independence.

One fact is certain about the monument: It is not a vanishing resource like open spaces or virgin forests. Mount Rushmore will stand for centuries as a reminder of the ideals of American democracy.

NOTES

Introduction

1. Quoted in William Zinsser, "Giants in Granite," *Travel Holiday*, February 1991, p. 75.
2. Quoted in *Time*, "Mountain Carver," March 17, 1941, p. 46.
3. Quoted in Donald Dale Jackson, "Gutzon Borglum's Odd and Awesome Portraits in Granite," *Smithsonian*, August 1992, p. 75.

Chapter 1: A Colossal Venture

4. Quoted in Rex Alan Smith, *The Carving of Mount Rushmore*. New York: Abbeville Press, 1985, p. 26.
5. Quoted in Gilbert Fite, *Mount Rushmore*. Norman: University of Oklahoma Press, 1952, p. 9.
6. Quoted in Smith, *The Carving of Mount Rushmore*, p. 24.
7. Quoted in Fite, *Mount Rushmore*, p. 9.
8. Quoted in Smith, *The Carving of Mount Rushmore*, p. 26.
9. Quoted in Fite, *Mount Rushmore*, p. 10.
10. Quoted in Fite, *Mount Rushmore*, p. 11.
11. Quoted in Smith, *The Carving of Mount Rushmore*, p. 27.
12. Fite, *Mount Rushmore*, p. 12.
13. Quoted in Lincoln Borglum, *Mount Rushmore: The Story Behind the Scenery*. Las Vegas: KC Publications, 1977, p. 7.
14. Quoted in Smith, *The Carving of Mount Rushmore*, p. 36.
15. Borglum, *Mount Rushmore*, p. 8.
16. Quoted in Smith, *The Carving of Mount Rushmore*, p. 96.
17. Quoted in Howard Shaff and Audrey Karl Shaff, *Six Wars at a Time: The Life and Times of Gutzon Borglum, Sculptor of Mount Rushmore*. Sioux Falls, SD: Center for Western Studies, Augustana College; Darien, CT: Permelia Publishing; Freeman, SD: Pine Hill Press, 1985, p. 230.

Chapter 2: Finances: A Problem from the Start

18. Quoted in Fite, *Mount Rushmore*, p. 58.
19. Quoted in Fite, *Mount Rushmore*, p. 60.
20. Quoted in Smith, *The Carving of Mount Rushmore*, p. 116.
21. Quoted in Smith, *The Carving of Mount Rushmore*, p. 119.
22. Quoted in Judith St. George, *The Mount Rushmore Story*. New York: G. P. Putnam's Sons, 1985, p. 50.

23. Borglum, *Mount Rushmore*, pp. 11–12.

24. *Popular Mechanics*, "Carving a Mountain to Tell Nation's Story," March 1927, p. 367.

25. Quoted in Shaff and Shaff, *Six Wars at a Time*, p. 243.

26. Quoted in Fite, *Mount Rushmore*, p. 75.

27. Quoted in Fite, *Mount Rushmore*, p. 75.

28. Quoted in Fite, *Mount Rushmore*, p. 76.

29. Quoted in Borglum, *Mount Rushmore*, p. 21.

30. Quoted in Fite, *Mount Rushmore*, p. 77.

31. Quoted in Fite, *Mount Rushmore*, p. 78.

32. Quoted in Fite, *Mount Rushmore*, p. 78.

Chapter 3: A Small Beginning

33. Quoted in Smith, *The Carving of Mount Rushmore*, p. 158.

34. Lincoln Borglum, *My Father's Mountain: Mt. Rushmore National Memorial and How It Was Carved*. Rapid City, SD: Fenwinn Press, 1965, p. 12.

35. Quoted in Smith, *The Carving of Mount Rushmore*, pp. 166–68.

36. Quoted in Fite, *Mount Rushmore*, p. 79.

37. Quoted in Borglum, *Mount Rushmore*, p. 31.

38. Quoted in St. George, *The Mount Rushmore Story*, p. 68.

Chapter 4: Government Comes to the Rescue

39. Quoted in Shaff and Shaff, *Six Wars at a Time*, p. 253.

40. Quoted in Shaff and Shaff, *Six Wars at a Time*, p. 253.

41. Quoted in Shaff and Shaff, *Six Wars at a Time*, p. 253.

42. Quoted in Shaff and Shaff, *Six Wars at a Time*, p. 261.

43. Quoted in Shaff and Shaff, *Six Wars at a Time*, p. 261.

44. Quoted in Shaff and Shaff, *Six Wars at a Time*, pp. 261–62.

45. Quoted in Borglum, *My Father's Mountain*, p. 3.

46. Quoted in St. George, *The Mount Rushmore Story*, p. 70.

47. Quoted in Shaff and Shaff, *Six Wars at a Time*, p. 269.

48. Quoted in Shaff and Shaff, *Six Wars at a Time*, p. 270.

49. Quoted in Fite, *Mount Rushmore*, p. 107.

50. Quoted in Smith, *The Carving of Mount Rushmore*, p. 212.

Chapter 5: Carving Continues

51. Quoted in Fite, *Mount Rushmore*, p. 119.

52. Quoted in Fite, *Mount Rushmore*, p. 119.

53. Borglum, *Mount Rushmore*, p. 40.

54. Quoted in Smith, *The Carving of Mount Rushmore*, p. 234.

55. Quoted in Fite, *Mount Rushmore*, p. 130.

56. Quoted in Smith, *The Carving of Mount Rushmore*, p. 286.

57. Quoted in Fite, *Mount Rushmore*, p. 141.

58. Quoted in Fite, *Mount Rushmore*, p. 155.

59. Quoted in Fite, *Mount Rushmore*, p. 160.

60. Quoted in Fite, *Mount Rushmore*, p. 170.

61. Quoted in St. George, *The Mount Rushmore Story*, p. 90.

62. Quoted in St. George, *The Mount Rushmore Story*, p. 92.

63. Quoted in Borglum, *My Father's Mountain*, p. 8.

64. Quoted in St. George, *The Mount Rushmore Story*, p. 98.

Chapter 6: Grand Plans Shatter

65. Quoted in Fite, *Mount Rushmore*, p. 214.

66. Quoted in Smith, *The Carving of Mount Rushmore*, pp. 362–63.

67. *Newsweek*, "Four Faces in Granite: Borglum's Black Hills Colossus Is Nearing Completion," July 10, 1939, p. 23.

68. Quoted in Fite, *Mount Rushmore*, p. 217.

69. Quoted in Fite, *Mount Rushmore*, p. 219.

70. Quoted in Smith, *The Carving of Mount Rushmore*, p. 373.

71. Quoted in St. George, *The Mount Rushmore Story*, p. 113.

Epilogue

72. Quoted in Borglum, *Mount Rushmore*, p. 34.

73. Borglum, *Mount Rushmore*, p. 43.

74. Quoted in Fite, *Mount Rushmore*, p. 233.

75. Quoted in Fite, *Mount Rushmore*, p. 233.

FOR FURTHER READING

Lincoln Borglum, *My Father's Mountain: Mt. Rushmore National Memorial and How It Was Carved.* Rapid City, SD: Fenwinn Press, 1965. Lincoln Borglum uses photographs and quotes to show the steps taken to create the Rushmore memorial.

Katherine M. Doherty and Craig A. Doherty, *Mount Rushmore.* Woodbridge, CT: Blackbirch Press, 1995. Written for younger readers, this book gives a brief overview of the building of the monument.

Judith St. George, *The Mount Rushmore Story.* New York: G. P. Putnam's Sons, 1985. This book details the events, people, and historical background of the national memorial.

T. D. Griffith, *America's Shrine of Democracy.* 1930. Reprint, Sioux Falls, SD: Modern Press, 1990. This book depicts the history of the carving of Mount Rushmore in numerous photographs.

WORKS CONSULTED

Books

Lincoln Borglum, *Mount Rushmore: The Story Behind the Scenery.* Las Vegas: KC Publications, 1977. Lincoln Borglum shares his memories of working at his father's side during the entire fourteen-year carving of Mount Rushmore.

Gilbert Fite, *Mount Rushmore.* Norman: University of Oklahoma Press, 1952. Considered by the National Park Service to be the "Bible" of facts about Mount Rushmore, this book presents a thorough discussion of events and the people involved in the building of the national memorial.

Howard Shaff and Audrey Karl Shaff, *Six Wars at a Time: The Life and Times of Gutzon Borglum, Sculptor of Mount Rushmore.* Sioux Falls, SD: Center for Western Studies, Augustana College; Darien, CT: Permelia Publishing; Freeman, SD: Pine Hill Press, 1985. This biography describes the man who devoted the last fourteen years of his life to creating Mount Rushmore and the details of this great adventure.

Rex Alan Smith, *The Carving of Mount Rushmore.* New York: Abbeville Press, 1985. Smith uses extensive quotes to tell the story of Mount Rushmore.

Periodicals

Gutzon Borglum, "Mountain Sculpture," *Scientific American,* January 1933. Borglum describes the then new method of using dynamite to remove stone from two memorials: Stone Mountain and Mount Rushmore.

M. Samuel Cannon and Gabriel Palkuti, "Who Was Gutzon Borglum?" *American History Illustrated,* December 1974. This is a pictorial essay on the life and times of the dedicated sculptor.

Daniel Chu, "About Faces," *People Weekly,* July 22, 1991. Chu quotes Sioux editor Tim Giago, who views Mount Rushmore as a symbol of dishonor.

Mark D. Coburn, "The Great Stone Faces," *Natural History,* January 1977. This author expresses his environmental concerns regarding sculpting a mountain.

Pat Dobbs, "Museum Caps Rushmore Makeover," Rapid City *Journal*, June 14, 1998. This article describes the formal opening of Mount Rushmore's renovated visitor facilities—primarily the new Lincoln Borglum Visitor Center and Museum.

————, "Records Vault Put in Place," Rapid City *Journal*, August 10, 1998. Four generations of Borglums fulfill the sculptor's dream to safeguard the history of America and the Rushmore monument by burying a time capsule in the uncompleted Hall of Records.

Paul Friggens, "America's Shrine of Democracy," *Reader's Digest*, August 1972. The four presidents carved in ageless granite remind readers of America's ideals.

Alex Heard, "Mount Rushmore: The Real Story," *New Republic*, July 15–22, 1991. This article exposes some of the foibles and criticisms behind the scenes in the building of the famous monument.

Miriam Horn, "Considering America's Heroes on a Human Scale," *U.S. News & World Report*, July 15, 1991. Borglum wanted people to know that these four presidents were ordinary men who served extraordinary ideals.

Donald Dale Jackson, "Gutzon Borglum's Odd and Awesome Portraits in Granite," *Smithsonian*, August 1992. This essay describes a feisty sculptor who spent fourteen years turning a South Dakota mountain into an oversized tribute to four presidents.

Richard Kaplan, "Mount Rushmore's Fantastic 'Facial,'" *Coronet*, December 1958. Exciting photos complement this article on one of the world's man-made wonders.

Life, "Saving Face," February 1990. A team of geologists made a three-dimensional computerized model of Mount Rushmore to study present and future cracks.

Newsweek, "Four Faces in Granite: Borglum's Black Hills Colossus Is Nearing Completion," July 10, 1939. This article describes the unveiling of Theodore Roosevelt, which brought the completion of the memorial near.

Popular Mechanics, "Carving a Mountain to Tell Nation's Story," March 1927. Borglum submitted photos of his model, and the article described his vision of the monument, including the entablature.

Rex Alan Smith, "Shrine of Democracy," *American History Illustrated*, July/August 1991. Smith describes Mount Rushmore as an inspiring monument to American presidents and their ideals, and he praises the men who created it.

Time, "Mountain Carver," March 17, 1941. Borglum was credited for having a talent for carving colossal objects.

USA Today, "Mount Rushmore: Monument to America," July 1991. This article is a pictorial account of the many phases of carving the memorial.

Nathan Ward, "1941: Fifty Years Ago—The Making of the Presidents," *American Heritage*, October 1991. This essay briefly discusses the carving of Rushmore and includes quotes from former monument workers.

William Zinsser, "Giants in Granite," *Travel Holiday*, February 1991. The author describes the fiftieth anniversary celebration of Mount Rushmore's heroic presidential figures.

Video Recordings

Jaffe Productions; Hearst Entertainment Television, *Mount Rushmore*. New York: A&E Home Video, 1994. This fifty-minute historical documentary about Mount Rushmore in the Black Hills of South Dakota includes interviews with a few surviving Mount Rushmore workers and National Park Service employees at Rushmore.

Bob Muller, executive producer, *Mount Rushmore, America in Stone*. Salisbury, MD: All American Video Productions, 1994. This forty-minute video details the story of Mount Rushmore's design, purpose, materials, dimensions, workers, and supporters.

INDEX

PICTURE CREDITS

ABOUT THE AUTHOR

Judith Janda Presnall enjoys traveling as part of the research for her books, and she found a personal visit to Mount Rushmore National Memorial particularly informative.

Presnall's other books published by Lucent include *Oprah Winfrey, The Giant Panda, Artificial Organs,* and *Rachel Carson.*

Both the Society of Children's Book Writers and Illustrators and the California Writers Club have recognized Presnall for her nonfiction writing. In 1997 she was honored with the Jack London Award for meritorious service by the California Writers Club, San Fernando Valley Branch.

Presnall was raised in Milwaukee, Wisconsin, and has earned a bachelor of education degree from the University of Wisconsin, Whitewater. Presnall and her husband, Lance, live in southern California with their three cats.